The Effect of Multinational Enterprises on Climate Change

The Effect of Multinational Enterprises on Climate Change

Supply Chain Emissions, Green Technology Transfers, and Corporate Commitments

Victor Steenbergen
Abhishek Saurav

WORLD BANK GROUP

1 2 3 4 26 25 24 23

ISBN (paper): 978-1-4648-1994-0
ISBN (electronic): 978-1-4648-1995-7
DOI: 10.1596/978-1-4648-1994-0

Cover design: Veronica Elena Gadea / World Bank

The Library of Congress Control Number has been requested.

Contents

Boxes

Figures

Maps

Tables

Foreword

The world is facing an urgent need to address climate change. Without urgency in action and emissions reductions across all sectors, limiting global warming to 1.5 degrees Celsius will not be possible. According to a 2022 IPCC report, global greenhouse gas emissions need to stabilize before 2025, be reduced by 43 percent by 2030, and reach net-zero by 2050. Only through immediate and coordinated action can we limit the damages from climate change and minimize the adverse effects of rising temperatures on growth, poverty reduction, and conflict around the world.

Climate action from both the public and private sectors is vital to meet this objective and accelerate the transition. In December 2015, 195 states signed the Paris Agreement. This pact provides an international agreement on tackling climate change that sets out each country's pledge to lower their emissions. While countries are increasingly taking steps to realize their commitments, there is a lack of consensus on how to translate global reduction targets into business-specific actions. Yet, private-sector engagement is critical to rapidly decarbonize existing supply chains and as a source of investment to accelerate the global energy transition.

This new report considers the impact of a key private sector player—multinational enterprises (MNEs)—on climate change. The report discusses the challenges and opportunities that MNEs pose to climate change mitigation by bringing together new data, empirical analysis, and the latest literature. Its findings show that a small number of MNEs are a major driver of global emissions, but also that these companies can quickly provide meaningful reforms to the emissions of their global suppliers by encouraging the use of green technologies and the adoption of sustainability standards. It also finds that MNEs offer an important source of investment for the climate transition, with an increasing share of foreign direct investment flowing into green sectors. Yet, the report also alerts us to the risk of inaction and resistance from MNEs, and it finds that many MNEs still have limited and insufficient corporate commitments to decarbonizing their own production and their supply chains.

Governments can and should do more to shape the behaviors of MNEs as part of their climate change mitigation plans, to help accelerate the climate transition. This report highlights how various policies can shape MNEs' impact on climate change by shaping their decisions to produce, invest, and engage in their network of affiliates and suppliers. These policy approaches include better monitoring firms' emissions, strengthening laws and regulations, changing price signals via tax policy and fiscal support, and using persuasion to guide the actions of MNEs, among others.

The race to net-zero is on. As governments are looking for ways to accelerate their transition to low-carbon economies, governments should utilize all the analytical and policy tools they can. In this light, *The Effect of Multinational Enterprises on Climate Change: Supply Chain Emissions, Green Technology Transfers, and Corporate Commitments* provides a useful and timely contribution to the discussion on climate change by shedding light on multinational enterprises as a major driver of global emissions. It is our hope that this report will help guide policy makers around the world and shape World Bank Group operations going forward.

Mona Haddad
Global Director for Trade, Investment, and Competitiveness
World Bank

Foreword

For the past 23 years, CDP has been laser focused on scaling the ambition of companies, cities, states, and regions measuring, disclosing, and acting on their environmental impact. This simple yet powerful goal has led global investors, businesses, and governments to provide a wealth of measurable data.

These data are crucial to understanding how we can respond to the climate crisis. CDP has evolved to become the only global, independent, environmental disclosure mechanism. CDP's annual cycle of interventions is now relied upon by financial institutions to make critical investment decisions, by buyers to work with their suppliers, and by policy makers to drive stronger environmental action.

From this vantage point, we can see that each company has its own story to tell. Disclosing data on emissions, water security, or deforestation is only the first step to change how a business is run for the better. This new report highlights the role that multinational enterprises (MNEs) play in promoting and guiding the urgent change that is needed.

Large MNEs can use their influence to embed low-carbon technologies in the markets in which they operate, to push their supply chains to adopt sustainability, and to finance climate mitigation and adaption. The flip side is that they could import their high-carbon habits and exacerbate the problem.

MNEs need national governments to work together to set stronger policies that will guide action on climate and nature issues. Many countries are developing strategies to build resilience against climate change and cut greenhouse gas emissions as quickly as possible. This report shows how MNEs need to be a partner in the net-zero transition, but it also shows that many of those with the highest emissions lack a clear, long-term plan to do something about it.

One of the striking, yet unsurprising, points to come out of this latest World Bank research, which analyzes CDP data, is how a handful of large corporates, and their supply chains, are responsible for the bulk of global industrial emissions. The outsized role these companies have acts both as a risk and an opportunity to mitigate the worst impacts of climate change, and their ambitions will determine the environmental performance of many countries.

Here again is where policy makers need to step in to show MNEs the way. As the analysis makes clear, shifting their effect on climate change will require a suite of policy instruments that includes implementing better emissions monitoring; setting strong standards; developing incentives to encourage green R&D; and imposing environmental taxes.

This important work reiterates the need to engage with these companies to better understand their activities and how they can shape the future of climate action.

Nicolette Bartlett
Chief Impact Officer
CDP

Acknowledgments

This report was developed by Victor Steenbergen (Senior Economist, World Bank Group) and Abhishek Saurav (Senior Economist). Extended team members include Kartik Akileswaran, Habtamu Tesfaye Edjigu, Ekaterina Grushko, Mauricio Alejandro Pinzon Latorre, and Thomas Ublackner. The report's interior design and typesetting were done by Ashley Young from Publications Professionals LLC. The report's cover was designed by Veronica Elena Gadea.

The report has benefited from the comments and suggestions from our colleagues: Somik Lall (Lead Economist), Thomas Farole (Lead Economist), John Gabriel Goddard (Lead Economist), Habib Rab (Lead Economist), Arti Grover (Senior Economist), and Trang thu Tran (Senior Economist). Special thanks also to CDP (formerly the Carbon Disclosure Project) for providing access to their firm-level emissions data that forms the basis for much of the analysis in this report.

This report was developed by the Investment Climate Unit of the World Bank. Mona Haddad, Global Director for Trade, Investment, and Competitiveness, and Asya Akhlaque, Finance, Competitiveness, and Innovation Global Practice Manager, provided guidance and supervision throughout.

About the Authors

Abhishek Saurav is a Senior Economist in the Finance, Competitiveness, and Innovation Global Practice of the World Bank Group. He advises governments on evidence-based design and implementation of policy reforms and development programs that catalyze investments and drive economic growth. He has a track record of leadership and innovation in development policy research, which includes the design of the Green Investment Climate Diagnostic (GICD) and the Global MNE Pulse Surveys of the World Bank Group. He has published and presented at international conferences on topics related to economic development, investments, environmental sustainability, and the impact of the COVID-19 (coronavirus) crisis. His experience spans developing regions in Africa, Asia, Europe, the Middle East, and the Americas. He holds a doctorate in public policy and public administration from The George Washington University, Washington, DC.

Victor Steenbergen is a Senior Economist in the Investment Climate Unit at the World Bank. His current work focuses on empirical research and policy advice related to the determinants and development impact of investment, with a special focus on trade, tax, and climate change mitigation policy. He recently coauthored *An Investment Perspective on Global Value Chains* and "Making the Most of the African Continental Free Trade Area" and has contributed analyses underlying several World Bank publications. Previously, he was Country Economist for the International Growth Centre in Rwanda, a public finance consultant in Nigeria, and an economist (ODI fellow) in the Budget Unit of Malawi's Ministry of Education. He holds a master's degree in public administration and development economics from the London School of Economics.

Main Messages

Multinational enterprises (MNEs) provide both a fundamental risk to and an opportunity for climate change mitigation. Proactive MNEs can impose sustainability standards or encourage green technology transfers that affect millions of producers and quickly reduce emissions. Yet, some MNEs may hold back emissions reduction by resisting, obstructing, or lobbying against change.

A small number of MNEs are a major driver of global greenhouse gas (GHG) emissions. This report's analysis suggests that the direct activities and supply chains of 157 large MNEs jointly account for up to 60 percent of global industrial emissions. While 10 percent comes from MNEs' direct activities, their supply chains account for another 50 percent of global emissions.

Most of the 157 MNEs are insufficiently committed to decarbonizing production and supply chains. Only one in four of all MNEs have committed to net-zero GHG emissions by 2050. Few have a long-term strategy (20 percent), a medium-term strategy (13 percent), or a short-term strategy (5 percent). None of the MNEs had a capital allocation strategy that aligned to net-zero emissions by 2050. The lack of short-term plans to decarbonize production and supply chains raises credibility concerns about the realism of MNEs' long-term commitments.

Yet, MNEs can help domestic firms decarbonize by providing access to more advanced, low-carbon technology. MNEs' production is less carbon-intensive than that of domestic firms. Firms that interact more with MNEs (via licensing, supply linkages, or joint ventures) are more likely to engage in green target-setting, monitoring, and decarbonization. This suggests MNEs can be an important part of the solution.

MNEs are increasingly shifting their new investments to green sectors and avoiding polluting sectors. Foreign direct investment (FDI) announcements in green sectors have strongly increased, rising by 700 percent between 2003 and 2021. In contrast, foreign investment in polluting sectors has declined by 80 percent over the same period. Green FDI has also overtaken FDI in polluting sectors. As a ratio, green and polluting FDIs' share shifted from 5-to-95 percent in 2003, to 66-to-34 percent in 2021. MNEs thus offer an important source of finance for the climate transition.

Countries should actively consider MNEs in their climate change mitigation plans. This report introduces a new framework, the 5Ps, which shows how various policies can shape MNEs' impact on climate change. The 5Ps are *patrolling* (monitoring emissions), *prescription* (laws and regulations), *penalties* (taxes), *payments* (incentives and fiscal support), and *persuasion* (corporate commitments and information). These tools can encourage MNEs to reduce emissions-intensive production, help them shift their supply chains to lower-carbon production methods, and facilitate the transition to a low-carbon industrial structure by attracting green FDI and phasing out dirty sectors.

Overview

Introduction

The world today confronts an unprecedented climate crisis, and governments zealously seek solutions: multinational enterprises (MNEs) should play a central role. Climate change is a defining challenge of our time—posing serious threats to countries' ability to secure past developments and sustainably achieve future improvements in living standards. So it is urgent that countries build the resilience of and be ready to adapt their people and economies to the effects of climate change in their development strategies, while also reducing greenhouse gas (GHG) emissions to mitigate damaging changes to the climate (World Bank Group 2021). The success of such strategies for global climate action will depend in part on the willingness of pivotal private actors to reform their behavior, ensuring widespread access to new technologies and increasing the global flow of investments. For each of these reasons, multinational enterprises should play a central role in climate change policy.

MNEs provide both a fundamental risk to and an opportunity for climate change mitigation. The climate ambitions of MNEs will affect the environmental performance of countries around the world. As a leading actor, proactive MNEs can impose sustainability standards or encourage green technology transfers that, in some cases, could affect millions of producers and accelerate the climate transition (Thorlakson, Zegher, and Lambin 2018). However, obstructive MNEs may equally hold back any progress to reduce a country's emissions via inaction or by actively resisting, obstructing, or lobbying against change.

MNEs also offer an important source of finance for sustainable development by supplying countries with foreign direct investment (FDI). Fulfilling the global commitments made in the Paris Agreement on climate change and achieving the Sustainable Development Goals (SDGs)[1] requires an acceleration in financing. The United Nations Conference on Trade and Development estimates that between US$550 billion and US$850 billion in capital investment is needed in developing countries annually to meet goals related to climate mitigation, while another US$80 billion to US$120 billion is needed for adaptation (UNCTAD 2014). The United Nations (UN) estimated an average annual SDG funding gap of US$2.5 trillion in developing countries (UNEP 2018). Together with public and other private investments, the cross-border investments of MNEs offer an important source of finance for sustainable development (OECD 2022).

The objective of this report is to study the effect of MNEs on climate change. Toward this goal, the report reviews the latest available data, conducts new empirical analysis, and summarizes pioneering literature. The report answers four key questions related to the relationship between MNEs and climate change:

- What effect do MNEs currently have on climate change, both through their own activities and through the emissions of their broader supply chains?
- How do MNEs shape the potential transfer of green technologies to domestic firms, and how do different types of interactions with MNEs stimulate such technology transfers?
- How committed are leading MNEs currently to transitioning their supply chains to net-zero emissions by 2050, and do they have long-, medium-, and short-range strategies to realize this?
- What types of policies can influence MNEs' effects on climate change?

Box O.1 provides a brief overview of the different datasets and methodologies used in this report.

BOX O.1 Overview of Key Datasets and Methodologies Used

To consider the effect of multinational enterprises (MNEs) on emissions (chapter 2), we provide new estimates aggregating firm-level data. We start with CDP's (formerly Carbon Disclosure Project) Full GHG (Greenhouse Gas) Emissions Dataset that includes over 6,400 firms. However, not all firms in the database are analyzed, as it is currently not possible to identify the full ownership status of firms (and so, to distinguish the effect of MNEs). As an alternative, we focus analysis on 157 very large MNEs identified by Climate Action 100+,[a] whose supply chains jointly make up most of the world's carbon emissions. Next, to understand how the global supply chains of these firms affect each country's emissions targets, we exploit Bureau Van Dijk's Orbis data on MNEs' global affiliate structure and financial performance. We use this to apportion each MNE's global emissions based on its affiliates' relative financial performance within the MNE. Finally, to identify each MNE's global or country-level emission share, we then compare its global or affiliate emissions to country-level emissions from the Organisation for Economic Co-operation and Development's (OECD) Annual Air Emission and Greenhouse Gas (GHG) Accounts.

To analyze how committed leading MNEs are to transitioning their supply chains to net-zero emissions by 2050 (chapter 4), we again focus on our analysis on the 157 very large MNEs identified by Climate Action 100+ and use their database to review the MNEs' overall climate commitment in the long-, medium-, and short-run. To review the country-level commitment of MNEs, we continue to exploit Orbis and CDP to apportion each MNE's global emissions to its MNE affiliates. We then consider the share of MNEs committed to a net-zero transition and weigh commitment based on their total emissions in the country.[b]

(Box continues on the following page.)

BOX 0.1 Overview of Key Datasets and Methodologies Used *(continued)*

We also consider how different interactions between domestic firms and MNEs shape the potential of green technology transfers to domestic firms (chapter 3). This analysis makes use of the World Bank Enterprise Survey's new Green Module, which is available for 36 countries (2018–20) and provides data about nine green firm characteristics using firms' strategic objectives and target setting, monitoring, and implementation measures. To consider the effect of MNE interactions, we conduct simple firm-level regressions based on foreign ownership, international supply links, and international licensing.

Table BO1.1 provides an additional summary of the various datasets and methodologies used in this report.

TABLE BO1.1 Overview of Key Datasets and Methodologies

Data	Key question	Methodology
• CDP's database provides carbon emissions data for 6,400+ firms. • Climate Action 100+ data identify 157 MNEs with the highest carbon emissions in the world and their overall climate commitments. • Orbis provides ownership (including MNEs' global affiliate structure) and financial information for over 140 million firms. • OECD's Emission and Greenhouse Gas database provides each country's total and sectoral carbon emissions.	What effect do MNEs have on the emissions of their supply chains? (chapter 2)	• Identify 157 large MNEs from Climate Action 100+ and detect their global emissions using CDP's database. • Use Orbis data to identify the global ownership structure and financial information of 157 large MNEs' to apportion global emissions across all their affiliates. • Estimate the global/country-level emissions share of 157 large MNEs by comparing their total emissions to OECD's Emission and Greenhouse Gas database.
	How committed are leading MNEs to transitioning their supply chains to net-zero emissions by 2050? (chapter 4)	• Consider the overall commitment of 157 large MNEs using Climate Action 100+ data. • Use Orbis data to consider the global ownership structure of 157 large MNEs and thereby consider the climate commitments of all their affiliates. • Categorize countries based on emissions shares of affiliates of 157 large MNEs (using CDP, Orbis, and OECD), as well as climate commitments of affiliates of 157 large MNEs (using Climate Action 100+ and Orbis).
World Bank Enterprise Survey's Green Economy Module provides data on nine green firm characteristics for 36 countries (2018–2020).	How do interactions with MNEs shape the potential of green technology transfers? (chapter 3)	• Regression analysis to consider how different interactions between domestic firms and MNEs (via investment, partnership, and trade) affect domestic firms' green technology transfers.

Sources: World Bank based on CDP 2022a, Climate Action 100+ Initiative, OECD's database.

a. For more details, see https://www.climateaction100.org/.

b. In this case, we assume that the emissions commitment of the MNE affiliate follows the ambitions set by the headquarters. However, going forward, it would also be important to monitor/review how host countries could shape the climate ambitions from MNE affiliates to ensure they either match or exceed headquarters' targets.

This report builds on the research and key policy initiatives from several international organizations that have focused on the sustainable investment aspects of MNEs. This includes the Organisation for Economic Co-operation and Development's (OECD) *FDI Qualities Policy Toolkit*,[2] which provides new insights on the ways FDI affects carbon emissions, while also offering policy recommendations to help governments attract FDI that contributes to decarbonization by reducing the emissions associated with foreign investments and inducing low-carbon spillovers to domestic firms (OECD 2022). UNCTAD's latest World Investment Reports have also included important new analysis on sustainable investment dynamics (UNCTAD 2021, 2022). To encourage investment for sustainable development, the World Trade Organization's (WTO) investment facilitation agreement also makes explicit mention of the aim to expand and retain FDI flows to achieve sustainable development goals (WTO 2021). Other notable initiatives include a toolkit on investment facilitation for sustainable investment from the Columbia Center on Sustainable Investment (Berger, Kagan, and Sauvant 2022), and the World Investment for Development Alliance (WIDA) which is a new global platform dedicated to promoting investment for sustainable development.[3]

This report complements the existing literature by bringing together a more detailed, firm-level perspective of the impact of MNEs on climate change and provides a new conceptual framework to scale up policy reforms. Due to data limitations, previous work on MNEs and climate change has been relatively high-level in nature. Analysis has often focused on aggregate investment flows in the energy sector (for example comparing the number of new greenfield FDI project[4] announcements in fossil fuels versus renewables; OECD 2022), or investment in financial products related to the "environmental, social and governance" (ESG) category (UNCTAD 2021, 2022). Little work has gone into directly observing the role that MNEs have on their global carbon emissions via their supply chains. Yet, new advances in data collection at the firm level[5] and country level[6] have enabled new analysis and provide important insights for policy makers on how MNEs shape climate change and affect green technology spillovers to domestic firms and allow policy makers to gauge MNEs' commitments to decarbonization. This report brings together much of these new data to provide a more detailed, firm-level perspective of the impact of MNEs on climate change. It also provides a new conceptual framework (which we refer to as "the 5 Ps"[7]) that highlights the policy tools that can help MNEs mitigate their impact on climate change. This framework can inform policy makers, while simultaneously shaping the World Bank's ongoing advisory services to improve countries' investment climate.

The Effect of Multinational Enterprises on Climate Change

MNEs affect climate change via three channels: scale effects, technology effects, and composition effects. The climate change literature has often presented the activities of MNEs either as a risk to increase emissions in developing countries by shifting their polluting activities to locations with limited environmental regulation (pollution haven), or as an opportunity to reduce emissions in developing countries by attracting cleaner technologies (pollution halo). However, this binary view is too simplistic. New analysis using micro- and macro-data on GHG emissions showcases that MNEs and FDI can simultaneously bring with them challenges and opportunities for climate change mitigation through these three key channels (OECD 2022):

- **Scale effect:** MNEs are major drivers of emissions. As they increase their production, their host country would likely also increase their total emissions.
- **Technology effect:** MNEs can diffuse low-carbon knowledge and technologies to domestic firms, which can thereby reduce a sector's average carbon intensity and reduce emissions.
- **Composition effect:** MNEs' FDI also changes industrial structure. This has an ambiguous effect on emissions, as FDI could shift resources toward low- or high-carbon intensity activities.

Related to the scale effect, this report finds that a small number of MNEs are a major driver of global GHG emissions (figure O.1). The total emissions of 157 large MNEs jointly account for up to 60 percent of total industrial emissions. While their own activities jointly account for (only) 10 percentage points of global industrial emissions, their supply chains could add up to another 50 percentage points of global emissions.[8]

FIGURE O.1 Global Industrial Emissions of the Supply Chains of Large MNEs, 2021

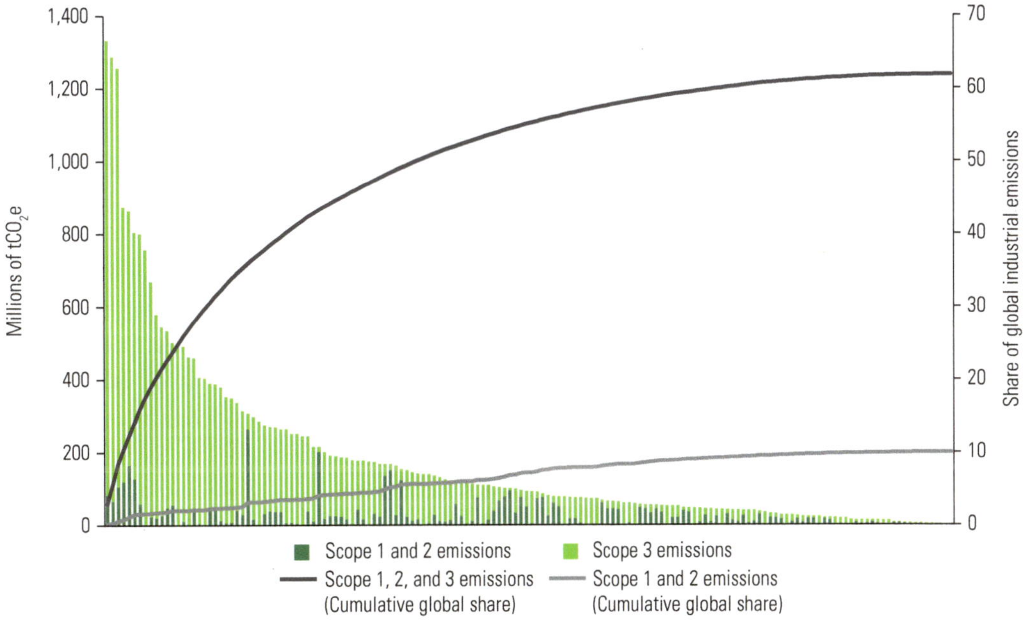

Sources: World Bank calculations based on CDP 2022a and OECD 2023.

Note: Scope 1 emissions are direct emissions from owned or controlled sources. Scope 2 emissions are indirect emissions from the generation of purchased electricity, steam, heating, and cooling consumed by the firm. Scope 3 emissions are all indirect emissions (not included in scope 2) that occur in the firm's value chain (see "Bottom-Up Approaches to Estimate the Effect of MNEs on Carbon Emissions" in chapter 2).). A total of 157 companies are identified based on Climate Action 100+. Each bar represents one MNE, while the lines show their own emissions as cumulative shares of global industrial emissions. CDP = formerly Carbon Disclosure Project; CO_2e = carbon dioxide equivalent; GHG = greenhouse gas; MNE = multinational enterprise; OECD = Organisation for Economic Co-operation and Development; t = tons of CO_2.

The affiliates of these 157 large MNEs make up a large share of emissions for many countries, while the most polluting sectors differ. We consider the network of MNE affiliates associated with these 157 large MNEs using Bureau Van Dijk's Orbis database. Our estimates suggest that their activities account for 1–25 percent of emissions in 85 countries, 25–50 percent of emissions in 9 countries, 50–75 percent in 8 countries, 75–100 percent in 9 countries, and over 100 percent of emissions in 25 countries (map O.1, panel a).[9] The energy sector tends to be the biggest polluter (via oil and gas, utility companies, or coal), but some regions dominate in transport, industrials, or consumer goods and services (map O.1, panel b).

New evidence also supports the technology effect, by finding that MNEs are considerably less carbon intensive in their production than domestic firms. Data from the CDP (formerly the Carbon Disclosure Project) Full GHG (Greenhouse Gas) Emissions Dataset find that in the case of steel, MNEs considerably overperform vis-à-vis domestic firms, producing somewhere between 18 and 48 percent fewer emissions for the same output (figure O.2, panel a). For cement, the results differ more significantly across product types. For clinkers, cement equivalent, and cementitious products, MNEs were able to produce the same goods for somewhere between 1 and 11 percent fewer emissions. Yet, in the case of low-carbon dioxide (CO_2) material, the average MNE was found to produce goods with 84 percent fewer emissions than domestic firms. Hence, while MNEs generally have a reduced carbon intensity of production in steel, for cement their advantage comes from the use of more sophisticated low-CO_2 products.[10] Overall, we find the dissemination of production technologies used by MNEs has significant potential to reduce the emissions of domestic firms.

FDI project announcements suggest that the composition effect of MNEs is improving, with FDI increasingly shifting out of polluting sectors and into green sectors. Greenfield FDI announcements for polluting sectors have gradually declined, while FDI is increasingly moving into green sectors (figure O.3, panel a). For international mergers and acquisitions, an increase in polluting sectors was followed by a significant decline. Firms in green sectors saw a substantial rise over time, so that in 2021 the value of green sector mergers and acquisitions (M&As) overtook that of polluting sectors (figure O.3, panel b). Global investment patterns have likely shifted for three main reasons. First, investors are reacting to rapidly declining costs and significant growth potential in renewable energy generation and low-carbon manufacturing methods (IRENA 2020). Second, companies are also responding to the rising pressures brought upon them by governments and investors and shareholders to engage in lower-carbon activities (World Bank, forthcoming). Third, shareholders have started to add a carbon risk premium at the firm level, which increases the cost of capital and raises the hurdle rates on new polluting investments (Bolton, Halem, and Kacperczyk 2022; Chava 2014). Jointly, this helps explain a growing number of green and slowing number of polluting greenfield FDI and cross-border M&A announcements over time.

MAP O.1 Emissions Associated with Affiliate Activities of Large MNEs, 2021

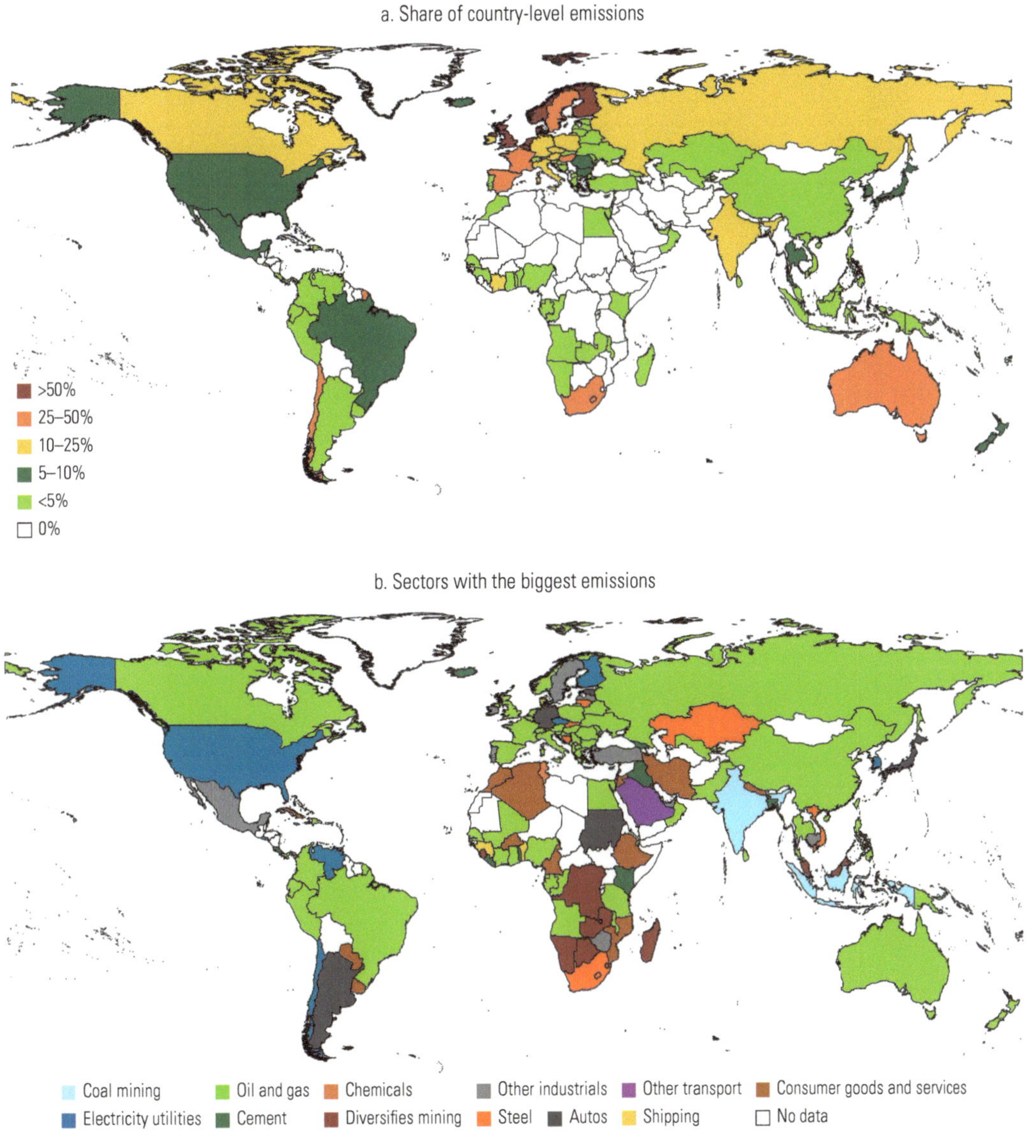

Sources: World Bank calculations based on CDP, Climate Action 100+, OECD, and Orbis data.

Note: 157 companies are identified based on Climate Action 100+. Because countries may partly export their carbon-intensive production abroad, MNE-based emissions can account for over 100 percent of country-reported emissions. CDP = formerly Carbon Disclosure Project; GHG = greenhouse gas; MNE = multinational enterprise; OECD = Organisation for Economic Co-operation and Development.

Decompositions further confirm that the scale, technology, and composition effects of MNEs changed over time (figure O.4). Zhang et al. (2020) suggest emissions from the global supply chains of MNEs have changed over time. They contributed to emissions between 2005 until 2011 (+20.4 percent) and 2008 until 2011 (+4 percent). The major contributing factor to this increase was the growth in the outputs of MNEs

FIGURE 0.2 Carbon Intensity of Production, Domestic Firms versus MNEs, 2021

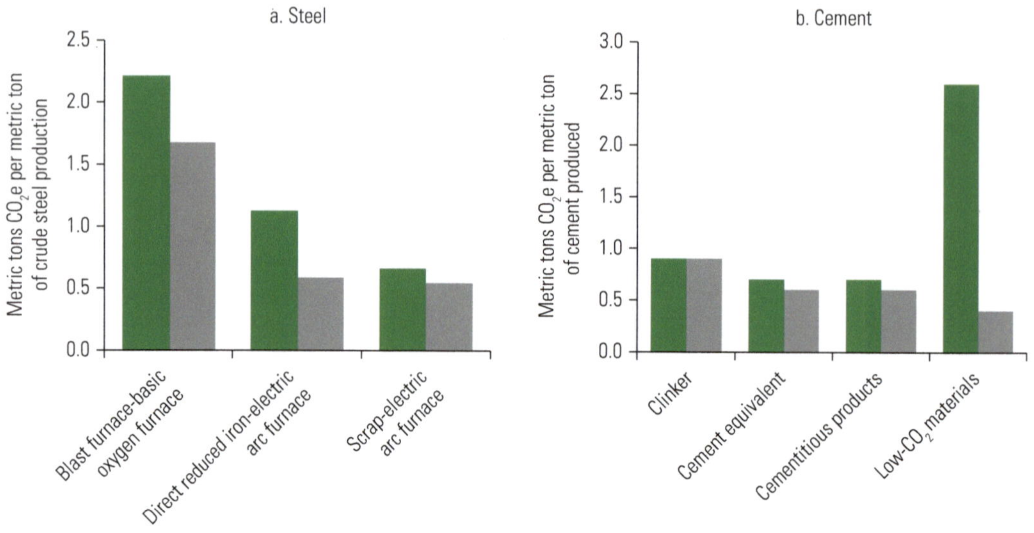

Source: World Bank estimates based on CDP Corporate Response Data.

Note: Figures on steel production are based on 28 companies: 14 MNEs and 14 domestic firms. Figures on cement production are based on 24 companies: 14 MNEs and 10 domestic firms. The firms' ownership characteristics (foreign/domestic) were manually identified using the Orbis' global ownership database. CDP = formerly Carbon Disclosure Project; CO_2e = carbon dioxide equivalent; MNE = multinational enterprise.

FIGURE 0.3 Green versus Polluting Global FDI Announcements, 2001–21

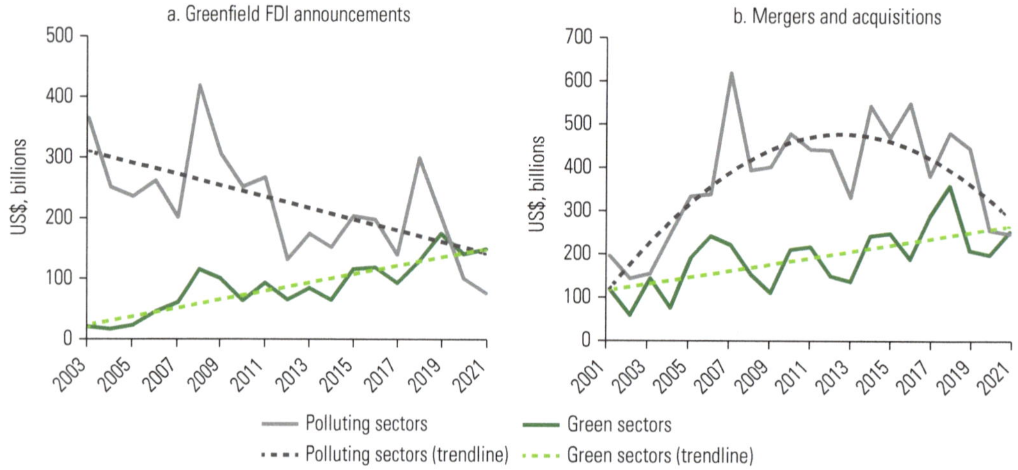

Sources: World Bank estimates using FDI markets and Refinitiv.

Note: Sectors classified in accordance with European Union Taxonomy for Sustainable Activities. The dotted lines provide the best-fitting trendlines. FDI = foreign direct investment.

FIGURE O.4 Emissions Embodied in the Supply Chains of MNEs: Scale, Technology, and Composition Effects

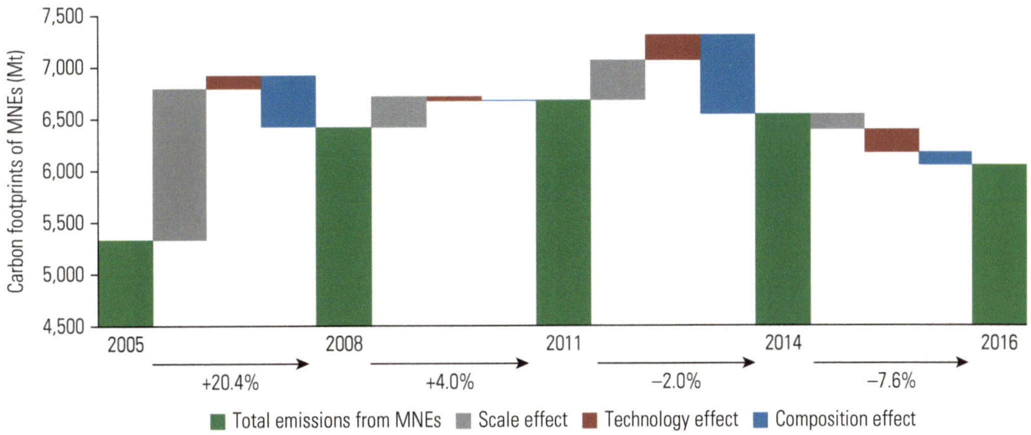

Source: World Bank based on Zhang et al. 2020.

Note: This analysis relies on a top-down approach to analyzing MNEs' carbon emissions that start from the International Energy Agency's country-sector emissions data, and combines that with the OECD's bilateral FDI stock data and the OECD's AMNE database that distinguishes the global trade patterns of MNEs and domestic firms in a Multi-Region Input-Output (MRIO) model. The results apply to 60 (mostly OECD) countries only. AMNE = Activities of Multinational Enterprises Database; FDI = foreign direct investment; MNE = multinational enterprise; Mt = metric tons; OECD = Organisation for Economic Co-operation and Development.

(scale effect), which would cause the carbon footprints of MNEs to increase by 27.4 percent in the absence of other factors. However, MNEs have since become a net reducer of carbon emissions. From 2011 to 2014, MNEs had a 2 percent decline in emissions. From 2014 to 2016 their carbon footprint declined by 7.6 percent. During this time, the scale effect, the technology effect, and composition effect all reduced the carbon footprints of MNEs. This is partly because the volume of global FDI shrunk, while MNEs began to adopt measures to reduce the carbon intensity of their supply chains, and gradually shifted toward lower-carbon activities (Zhang et al. 2020). This, in turn, shows the important (and sometimes countervailing) effects of the three channels: scale, technology, and composition.

Multinational Enterprises and Green Technology Transfers

Domestic firms that interact more with MNEs are engaged in more green actions (figure O.5). We conducted firm-level regressions using the World Bank's Enterprise Surveys' green module that considers firms' target setting, emissions monitoring, and specific actions (implementation measures) to reduce carbon emissions. We find statistically significant results that domestic firms linked to MNEs are more likely to adopt green business practices if they engage in equity partnerships (or FDI), supply links (or indirect exports), or technological licensing arrangements with MNEs, as compared to their peers without such links to MNEs. In general, international technology licensing is found to have the most sizeable effects, followed by international supply links.

FIGURE O.5 The Effect of MNE Links on Green Business Practices

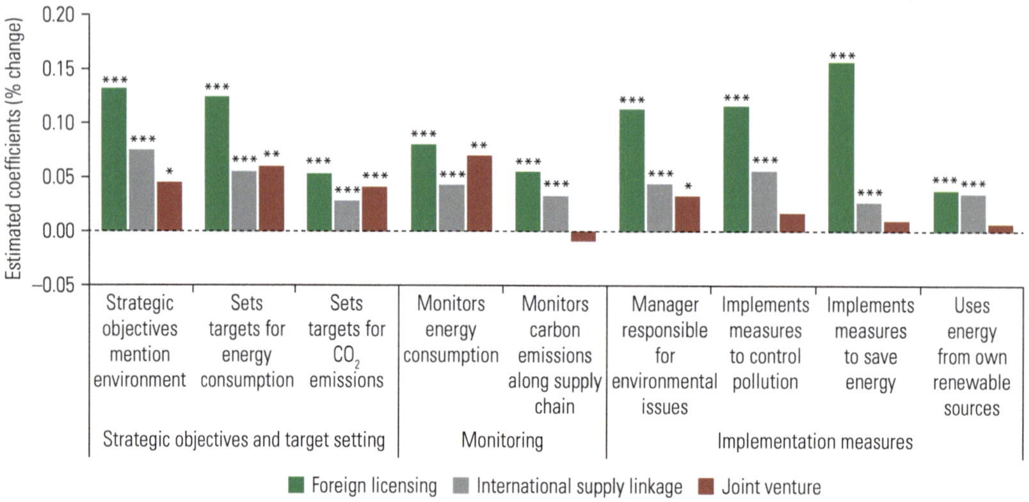

Source: World Bank calculations based on data from the World Bank Enterprise Survey 2020.

Note: Results are from individual regression, summarized in table 3A.1 in annex 3A. Each regression controls for country, sector, and year fixed effects as well as firm age and size. Parentheses report robust standard errors. Coefficients are described as marginal effects. CO_2 = carbon dioxide. MNE = multinational enterprise. * $p < 0.10$, ** $p < 0.05$, *** $p < 0.01$.

While joint ventures raise the likelihood of adopting green strategic objectives and monitoring, they generally did not increase the likelihood of domestic firms implementing measures to improve their environmental performance.

Government pressure remains a key lever for MNEs to encourage green technology transfers and increase investment in sustainability-enhancing activities. The presence of externalities and information asymmetries can distort MNE behavior and may hinder investments in green technologies or the dissemination of technologies within global supply chains. Government pressure remains key to stimulating green technology transfers. New evidence from the World Bank's *Global Investment Competitiveness Report 2021/2022* (GIC) survey suggests that firms are much more likely to invest in sustainability initiatives when experiencing pressure from governments (figure O.6).

The Climate Commitments of MNEs

In most countries, MNEs have not formally committed to transition to net-zero GHG emissions by 2050 (map O.2). In only eight countries have over 75 percent of large MNEs committed to transition to net-zero emissions by 2050, and these are all based in Europe. Another seven countries in Europe and East Asia have between 25 and 50 percent of large MNEs committed to net-zero. Most large MNEs headquartered in other regions, such as North America, South America, Africa, or the rest of Asia are all still uncommitted to net-zero by 2050.

FIGURE O.6 Key Drivers for MNEs to Invest in Sustainability Initiatives

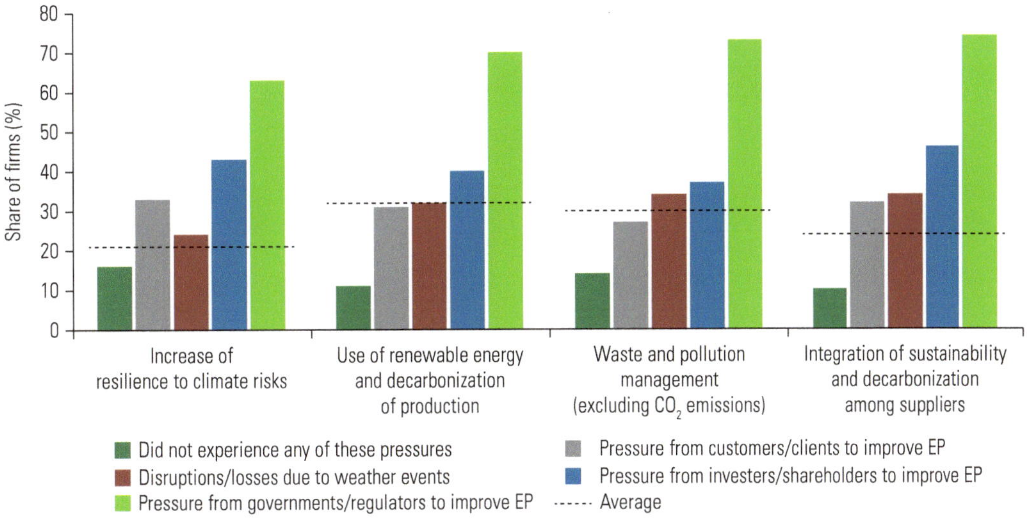

Source: World Bank calculations based on GIC 2021/2022 survey data (World Bank, forthcoming).

Note: This figure indicates the percentage of firms that are planning to increase their investment in environmentally sustainable initiatives. The number of observations = 1,060. CO_2 = carbon dioxide; EP = environmental performance; GIC = Global Investment Competitiveness; MNE = multinational enterprise.

MAP O.2 Share of MNEs Committed to Net-Zero GHG Emissions by 2050, by Headquarters Location

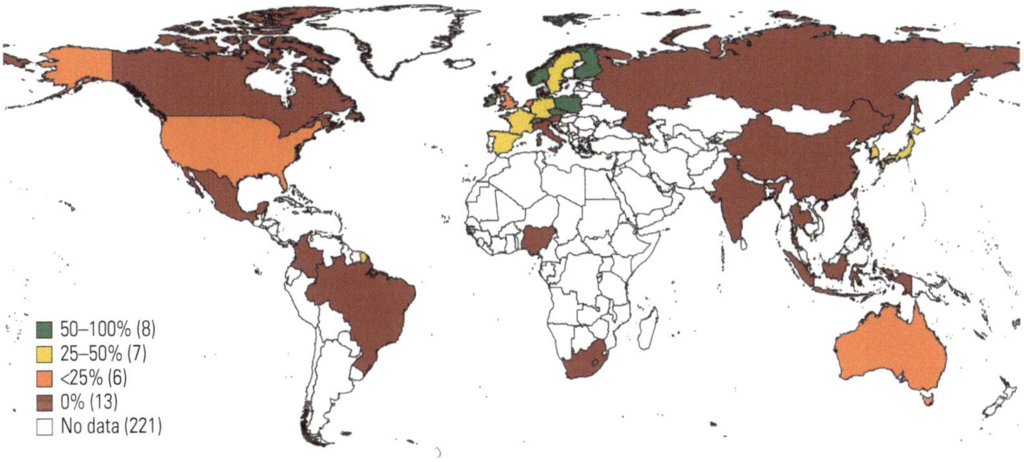

Source: World Bank calculations based on Climate Action 100+ data.

Note: The 157 companies are identified based on Climate Action 100+. Numbers in parentheses are the number of countries. GHG = greenhouse gas; MNE = multinational enterprise.

To better understand the potential risks and opportunities associated with the actions of large MNEs, we categorize countries based on MNEs' emission shares and climate commitment. From this, we derive four quadrants (map O.3):

1. **High MNE emissions share, high MNE commitment.** These large MNEs are critical but committed to change—thus forming a significant opportunity to accelerate a country's emissions reduction. Policy makers could collaborate with such MNEs to realize their stated objectives. This is the case in eight countries (all in Europe).
2. **Low MNE emissions share, high MNE commitment.** These large MNEs are less critical as a source of emissions, but they are still committed—thus forming some opportunity for reform. Countries could leverage these MNEs' goodwill to accelerate technology transfers that could help domestic firms decarbonize their production. We identify this for 25 countries located in Africa, Central Asia, Europe, and South America.
3. **Low MNE emissions share, low MNE commitment.** These large MNEs are neither a very critical source of emissions, nor are they very committed. This presents some risk, as polluting firms could lock the country into a high-emissions future. Yet given their limited role, there may be more urgent issues to focus on for climate mitigation. We identify 43 countries where this is the case, spread across Africa, Central Asia, Europe, and Latin America.

MAP O.3 Country-Level Emissions Share and Commitments to Climate Action of Large MNEs' Affiliates

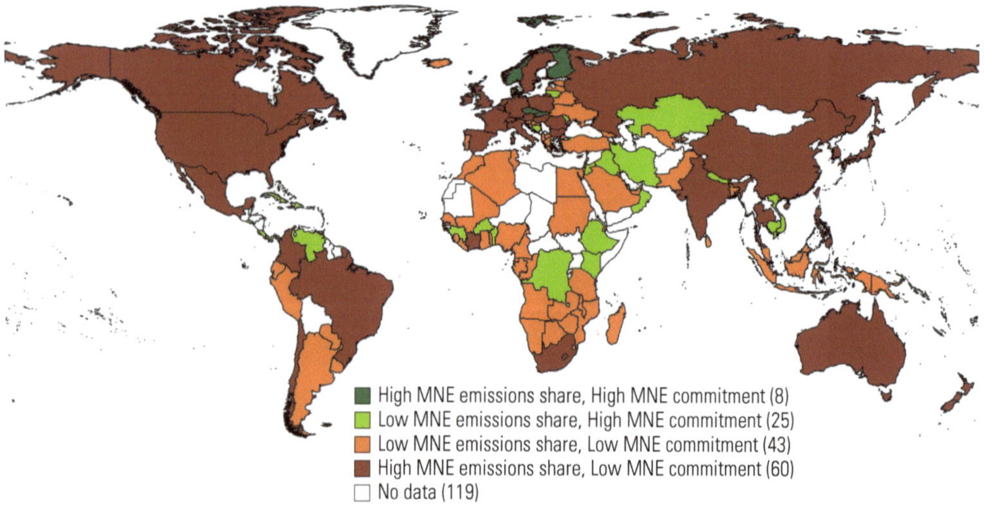

Sources: World Bank calculations based on CDP, Climate Action 100+, OECD, and Orbis data.

Note: Map shows the emissions-weighted share of firms that have committed to net-zero emissions by 2050. Numbers in parentheses are the number of countries. CDP = formerly Carbon Disclosure Project; MNE = multinational enterprise; OECD = Organisation for Economic Co-operation and Development.

4. **High MNE emissions share, low MNE commitment.** These MNEs are a significant risk to countries' climate change ambitions because they constitute a large share of emissions but display weak commitment for reform. To meet the country's climate targets, policy makers have a strong case for public intervention to encourage MNEs to adopt climate reforms. Worryingly, this is the case for 60 countries (the highest share of the four quadrants), including some of the world's most polluting countries.

Even more worrying, MNE commitments quickly decrease as firms are asked to shift their long-term strategies into long-, medium-, and short-term plans. Only one in four of all MNEs have a long-term strategy like net-zero GHG emissions by 2050 (figure O.7, panel a). Yet, the share of firms with such targets quickly drops for having a long-term strategy (20 percent), a medium-term strategy (13 percent), a short-term strategy (5 percent), or a decarbonization strategy (8 percent).[11] None of the MNEs had a capital allocation strategy that was formally aligned to net-zero emissions by 2050. The lack of tangible plans to decarbonize production and supply chains in the short-term further raises credibility concerns about the realism of MNEs' long-term commitments.

MNEs from high-income countries are more committed to the net-zero targets than developing countries. MNEs headquartered in high-income countries are more committed to net-zero targets (30 percent), while none of the MNEs headquartered in developing countries have formally committed themselves to net-zero targets (figure O.7, panel b). Yet the lagging nature of some big high-income countries (most notably Australia, Canada, and the United States—as shown in map O.3) illustrates that many high-income countries still face a considerable lack of MNE commitment.

MNEs in the consumer goods and services sectors are more committed than those in the industrials, transportation, or energy sectors (figure O.7, panel c). This in itself is likely also a reflection of the market structure faced by each of these sectors. For example, energy companies will face considerably more difficulty in transitioning to net-zero emissions than consumer goods sectors, and in some cases this transition is wholly unviable (for example in coal mining).

More broadly, the literature finds evidence of a deeper problem of companies intentionally giving an overly flattering representation of their climate actions ("greenwashing"). We briefly consider the causes of greenwashing and suggest how this can be avoided through more explicit external scrutiny. To limit corporate greenwashing requires more explicit initiatives to increase corporate disclosure of climate commitments and actions, greater standardization of emissions disclosure, and ideally, oversight by third-party actors to oversee and validate climate target-setting and action.

FIGURE 0.7 The Long-, Medium-, and Short-Term Commitment of 157 Large MNEs to Climate Action

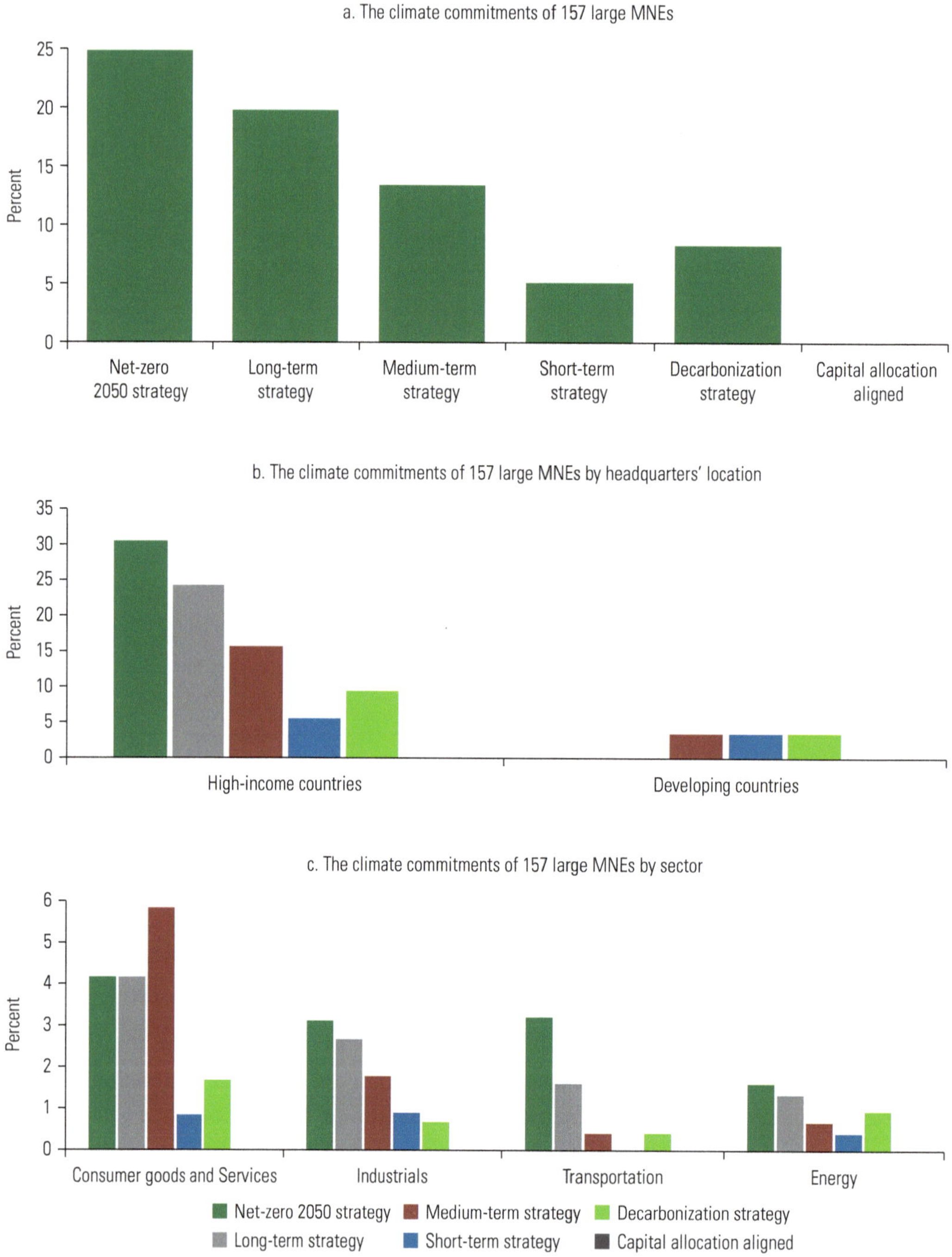

Source: World Bank calculations using Climate Action 100+ data.

Note: Long-term strategy covers the period between 2036 and 2050, medium-term strategy covers the period between 2026 and 2035, and short-term strategy covers the period up to 2025. Out of the 157 MNEs, 128 are headquartered in high-income countries, and 29 in developing countries. MNE = multinational enterprise.

Policies to Influence MNEs' Effect on Climate Change

Policy makers can use a range of policy tools (which we refer to as the 5Ps) to help MNEs mitigate their impact on climate change and better stimulate green growth (figure O.8). The 5Ps framework provides a useful way to identify the various types of instruments available to governments to affect the impact of MNEs on climate change. These tools can encourage MNEs to reduce emissions-intensive production (scale), help MNEs shift their supply chains to lower-carbon production methods (technology), and facilitate a shift toward a low-carbon industrial structure by attracting green FDI and phasing out dirty sectors (composition). Each approach has several policy instruments to affect scale, technology, and composition channels of MNEs on climate change (table O.1).

While the 5Ps instrument could be applied to all firms, large MNEs (and their supply chains) have specific characteristics that mean they may deserve special attention through both the choice of policy instruments and careful design of climate change policies. Two main elements set MNEs apart. First, their supply chain likely accounts for a disproportionate share of a country's emissions, so that MNEs will likely bear the brunt of most climate change policies (via any of the 5Ps). Second, MNEs often hold considerable bargaining power over host countries because they are less unrestricted than domestic firms and can threaten to shift their operations abroad (or to limit any

FIGURE O.8 Policy Approaches to Influence MNEs' Effect on Climate Change (the 5Ps Framework)

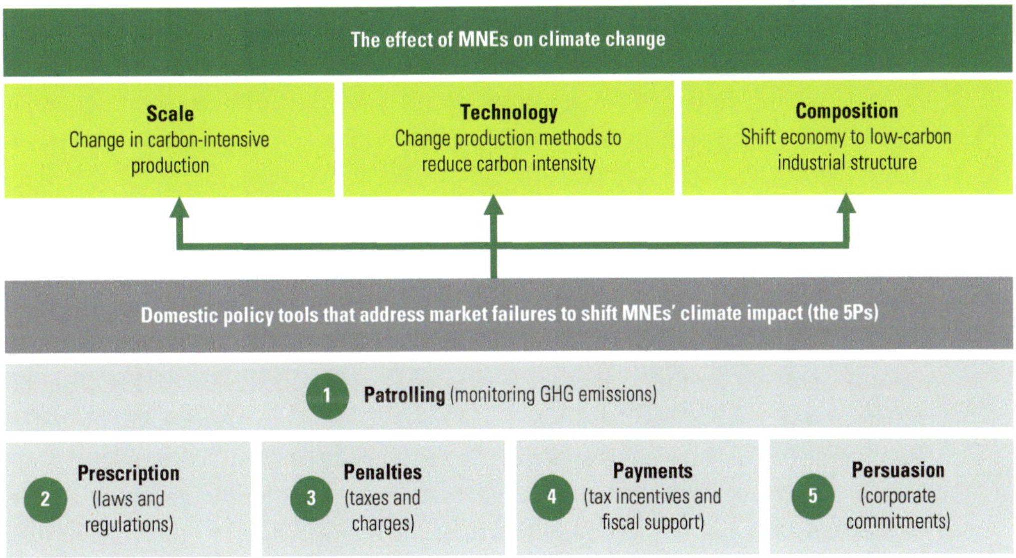

Sources: World Bank based on Grossman and Kruger 1991; Mandle et al. 2019.
Note: GHG = greenhouse gas; MNE = multinational enterprise.

TABLE O.1 Specific Instruments to Improve MNEs' Effect on Climate Change (the 5Ps Framework)

Domestic policy tools	Objectives to improve MNEs' effect on climate change mitigation		
	Scale channel Reduce carbon-intensive production	**Technology channel** Change production methods to reduce carbon intensity	**Composition channel** Shift economy toward a low-carbon industrial structure
Patrolling (monitoring emissions)	• Monitoring firm-level GHG emissions (scope 1, scope 2, and scope 3) • Voluntary reporting standards and environmental disclosure laws		
Prescription (laws and regulations)	• Environmental standards • Emission permits	• Environmental standards • Streamlined regulations for technology licensing, joint ventures, local sourcing	• Restrictive business/FDI regulation for polluting sectors • Liberalized business/FDI regulation for green sectors
Penalties (taxes and charges)	• Environmental taxes	• Environmental taxes	• Higher income tax for polluting sectors
Payments (tax incentives and fiscal support)	• Buyout plans	• Incentives for green R&D, skills training, capital upgrades • Incentives for technology licensing, JVs, supplier programs	• Tax incentives for green sectors.
Persuasion (corporate commitment and information campaigns)	• Corporate commitment campaigns	• Supply chain eco-certification • ESG/Impact investing • Investor aftercare on green reinvestment/supplier links	• Green investment promotion and facilitation

Source: World Bank based on literature review.

Note: Scope 1 emissions are direct emissions from owned or controlled sources. Scope 2 emissions are indirect emissions from the generation of purchased electricity, steam, heating, and cooling consumed by the firm. Scope 3 emissions are all indirect emissions (not included in scope 2) that occur in the firm's value chain (see "Bottom-Up Approaches to Estimate the Effect of MNEs on Carbon Emissions" in chapter 2). ESG = environmental, social, and governance; FDI = foreign direct investment; JV = joint venture; MNE = multinational enterprise; R&D = research and development.

future FDI). Jointly, this means that countries may want to pay special attention to MNEs in their policy framework, both through the choice of policy instruments and careful design to ensure the right balance so that MNEs (a) decarbonize their in-country supply chains, (b) collaborate more with domestic firms to encourage green transfers, and (c) do not feel so pressured that they choose to pull out of the country (and take with them particularly worthwhile capital, jobs, and technology). This report thus reviews the literature to discuss the MNE-related concerns across the 5Ps relevant for developing climate change policy.

Finally, this report calls for an active research agenda to further define how to prioritize, sequence, and implement economic policy to shape the climate change activities of MNEs. This report provides an overview of some of the latest literature, data, and economic analysis on the various challenges and opportunities that MNEs bring to climate change mitigation. It also touches on the various policy instruments available to policy makers in shaping this dynamic, via the 5Ps framework, and their relationship to scope, technology, and composition effects of MNEs. Yet there is still much that is unclear, most notably, how the various instruments complement or substitute for one another. To further inform this, box O.2 sets out a potential future research agenda on MNEs and climate change. This work will be critical going forward to guide policy makers in making the climate change transition by shaping the activities of MNEs.

BOX 0.2 Future Research Agenda

Strengthen Estimates of MNEs' Effect on Emissions by Harmonizing Top-Down and Bottom-Up Approaches

Chapter 2 provides an initial assessment of the effect of multinational enterprises (MNEs) on climate change. It argues that to better understand the role of MNEs in climate change, there could be significant benefits to harmonizing top-down and bottom-up approaches. The top-down approaches have the benefit of avoiding double-counting emissions within supply chains. Yet, they currently cannot differentiate the carbon intensity of MNEs and non-MNEs at the country-industry level. Bottom-up approaches that use firm-level data can enable estimation models to reflect the differences in carbon intensity between different groups of firms, such as between MNEs and non-MNEs, and across sectors. This type of approach would therefore utilize the best of both worlds; avoiding double counting of emissions across supply chains but incorporating heterogenous firm-level dynamics for the biggest firms across each country and industry. Jointly, this could likely provide the most accurate and realistic estimates of the role of MNEs on climate change.

Expand Firm-Level Data on Climate Change Mitigation and Adaption

Chapter 3 reflects on the role of the potential for green technology transfers. For this, it uses the World Bank Enterprise Survey's Green Economy Module, which provides valuable insights into firms' decisions on green strategic objectives and target setting, monitoring, and implementation measures. Yet, the data are available for only a few dozen countries, preventing more substantial analysis. Future advances in research that rely on primary data at the firm level as well as the Enterprise Survey could expand both geographical and topical coverage. For example, in addition to rolling out the Green Economy Module in more countries, the surveys should also sharpen the topical focus on climate change. This could include collecting information on the following:

- The strategies adopted by firms to raise environmental sustainability, such as management practices for production efficiency, resource use through circular economy practices, green innovation, and adoption of clean technologies, as well as the effect of such strategies on productivity and firm competitiveness;
- The current challenges faced by firms related to climate change and the potential technology and government policies that could help them adapt and strengthen their resilience; and
- The investment needs and challenges faced by firms in adopting clean technologies and practices, lowering their supply chain emissions, undertaking the process of reengineering, and other initiatives.

Monitor MNEs' Climate Change Reform Commitments in Headquarters and Host Countries

Chapter 4 considers the climate commitments of MNEs. This mostly relied on the stated climate ambitions set out by MNEs' headquarters, which was assumed to also apply to the MNEs' broader affiliate structure. Going forward, this analysis can be improved in three ways.

(Box continues on the following page.)

BOX 0.2 Future Research Agenda (continued)

- First, there is a need to monitor the actual behavior of MNEs in closer detail and consider whether more ambitious climate commitments result in more active reforms or whether this is "cheap talk" (see "Weaknesses in Corporate Climate Reporting and Greenwashing" in chapter 4).
- Second, more work is needed to consider how MNE affiliates follow the climate ambitions and actions of their headquarters, as it is possible that the emissions commitment of MNE headquarters and MNE affiliates in foreign countries differ systematically.
- Third, with access to more granular data on climate change ambitions and actions, researchers could further explore what may be driving these dynamics. Of particular importance would be to consider how environmental regulation in MNE headquarters as well as host countries may shape the actions of MNEs and their affiliates.

Use Specific and Complementary Policies to Shape the Impacts of MNEs on Climate Change

Chapter 5 touches on a range of policy instruments available to policy makers in shaping the impacts of MNEs on climate change, via the 5Ps framework and their relationship to scope, technology, and composition effects of MNEs. However, climate action and achieving impact through government programs require a more nuanced understanding of the mechanisms of impact and the contextual suitability of the 5Ps. Various knowledge deficiencies prevent such advancements, including the following:

- What insights can be found related to the policy responses being adopted by developed and developing countries for climate change mitigation and adaptation?
- To what extent do policy instruments complement each other? For example, patrolling is likely an important foundation for many of the other 5Ps.
- To what extent can instruments be substitutes in realizing similar objectives by affecting levers for behavior change? For example, regulations, taxes, and subsidies offer different ways to reach the same goal, which is typically a change in agent behavior.

Toward this end, a database that sources global information and is organized per the 5Ps framework could be of great value for policy researchers as well as policy makers.

Source: World Bank.

Notes

1. SDG Goal 13 relates to climate action and calls for urgent action to combat climate change and its impacts.
2. The FDI Qualities Policy Toolkit is designed to help governments identify priorities for policy reforms to strengthen FDI impacts in four SDG areas: productivity and innovation; job quality and skills; gender equality; and decarbonization.
3. See https://www.widalliance.org/ for more details.
4. Greenfield FDI refers to investments where a parent company establishes or expands a subsidiary in a foreign country—as opposed to mergers and acquisitions, which occur when a company purchases or leases an existing facility from another company.

5. Most notably CDP's Full GHG Emissions Dataset (see "Bottom-Up Approaches to Estimate the Effect of MNEs on Carbon Emissions" in chapter 2), the World Bank's Enterprise Survey's Green Module (see chapter 3), and Climate Action 100+ (see chapter 4).
6. Especially the OECD's AMNE database, as exploited by Zhang et al. (2020), Borga et al. (2022), and Zhu, Guo, and Zhang (2022). See "Top-Down Approaches to Estimate the Effect of MNEs on Carbon Emissions" in chapter 2.
7. The 5Ps are patrolling (monitoring emissions), prescription (laws and regulations), penalties (taxes), payments (incentives and fiscal support), and persuasion (corporate commitments and information).
8. This is an upper-bound estimate, based on aggregating the scope 3 emissions from MNEs. This could lead to double-counting emissions from multiple firms in the same value chain (for example, emissions from electricity use could be attributed to an energy company and a downstream metal smelting company). As such, aggregated scope 3 estimates should be interpreted with caution. Top-down approaches avoid double counting within supply chains (see "Top-Down Approaches to Estimate the Effect of MNEs on Carbon Emissions" in chapter 2.) and provide lower estimates of MNEs' effect on climate change, but are also narrower in defining firm-level climate impacts (for example, they do not account for emissions from final consumption).
9. Because countries may partly export their carbon-intensive production abroad, MNE-based emissions can account for over 100 percent of country-reported emissions.
10. These estimates are purely descriptive and do not control for the MNEs' larger firm size, which could drive the results. That said, the results may be underestimating MNEs' effect on carbon intensity. This is because the sample mostly includes firms that voluntarily include themselves in CDP's emissions database. Such firms tend to be larger and more committed to climate change mitigation and to have lower carbon intensity than the universe of firms (Bolton, Halem, and Kacperczyk 2022).
11. Long-term covers the period between 2036 and 2050, medium-term covers the period between 2026 and 2035, and short-term covers the period up to 2025.

References

Berger, Axel, Yardenne Kagan, and Karl P. Sauvant, eds. 2022. *Investment Facilitation for Development: A Toolkit for Policymakers,* 2nd ed. Geneva: International Trade Center (ITC). https://doi.org/10.2139/ssrn.3830031.

Bolton, P., Z. Halem, and M. Kacperczyk. 2022. "The Financial Cost of Carbon." *Journal of Applied Corporate Finance* 34: 17–29. https://doi.org/10.1111/jacf.12502.

Borga, M., A. Pegoue, G. Henri, A. Sanchez, D. Entaltsev, and K. Egesa. 2022. "Measuring Carbon Emissions of Foreign Direct Investment in Host Countries." International Monetary Fund (IMF) Working Paper WP/22/86, IMF, Washington, DC.

CDP (formerly the Carbon Disclosure Project). 2022a. *CDP Full GHG Emissions Dataset 2022: Summary.* CDP, London. https://www.cdp.net/en/investor/ghg-emissions-dataset.

CPD (formerly the Carbon Disclosure Project). 2022b. CDP Corporate Response Data.

Chava, S. 2014. "Environmental Externalities and Cost of Capital." *Management Science* 60 (9): 2223–47.

Grossman, G. M., and A. G. Kruger. 1991. "Environmental Influences of a North American Free Trade Agreement." Working paper 3914, National Bureau of Economic Research (NBER), Cambridge, MA.

IRENA (International Renewable Energy Agency). 2020. "How Falling Costs Make Renewables a Cost-Effective Investment." https://www.irena.org/newsroom/articles/2020/Jun/How-Falling-Costs-Make-Renewables-a-Cost-effective-Investment.

Mandle, L., Z. Ouyang, J. Salzman, and G. C. Daily, eds. 2019. *Green Growth That Works: Natural Capital Policy and Finance Mechanisms around the World.* Washington, DC: Island Press.

OECD (Organisation for Economic Co-operation and Development). 2022. *FDI Qualities Policy Toolkit.* Paris: OECD Publishing. https://doi.org/10.1787/7ba74100-en.

Thorlakson, T., J. F. de Zegher, and E. F. Lambin. 2018. "Companies' Contribution to Sustainability through Global Supply Chains." *Proceedings of the National Academy of Sciences* 115 (9): 2072–77. https://doi.org/10.1073/pnas.1716695115.

UNCTAD (United Nations Conference on Trade and Development). 2014. *World Investment Report 2014—Investing in the SDGs: An Action Plan.* Geneva: UNCTAD.

UNCTAD (United Nations Conference on Trade and Development). 2021. *World Investment Report 2021—Investing in Sustainable Recovery.* Geneva: UNCTAD.

UNCTAD (United Nations Conference on Trade and Development). 2022. *World Investment Report 2022—International Tax Reforms and Sustainable Investment.* Geneva: UNCTAD.

UNEP (United Nations Environment Programme). 2018. *Towards a Pollution-Free Planet: Background Report.* Nairobi: UNEP.

World Bank. Forthcoming. *Global Investment Competitiveness Report 2021/2022: Examining the Potential of Foreign Investment in a Green, Resilient, and Inclusive Economic Recovery.* Washington, DC: World Bank.

World Bank Group. 2021. *World Bank Group Climate Change Action Plan 2021–2025: Supporting Green, Resilient, and Inclusive Development.* Washington, DC: World Bank.

WTO (World Trade Organization). 2021. "Joint Statement on Investment Facilitation for Development," WT/L/1130, December 10, 2021. WTO, Geneva.

Zhang, Z., D. Guan, R. Wang, J. Meng, H. Zheng, K. Zhu, and H. Du. 2020. "Embodied Carbon Emissions in the Supply Chains of Multinational Enterprises." *Nature Climate Change* 10 (12): 1096–101.

Zhu, K., X. Guo, and Z. Zhang. 2022. "Reevaluation of the Carbon Emissions Embodied in Global Value Chains Based on an Inter-Country Input-Output Model with Multinational Enterprises." *Applied Energy* 307: 118220.

Abbreviations

ADB	Asian Development Bank
AMNE	Activity of Multinational Enterprises
ASEAN	Southeast Asian Nations
ACWI	All-Country World Index
CCSM	Corporate Climate Sustainability Monitor
CDP	Carbon Disclosure Project
CO_2	carbon dioxide
CO_2e	carbon dioxide equivalent
EPA	Environmental Protection Agency (United States)
ESG	environmental, social, and governance
EU	European Union
FDI	foreign direct investment
5Ps	patrolling (monitoring emissions), prescription (laws and regulations), penalties (taxes), payments (incentives and fiscal support), and persuasion (corporate commitments and information)
GDP	gross domestic product
GHG	greenhouse gas
GIC	*Global Investment Competitiveness Report*
GVCs	global value chains
ICIO	Inter-Country Input-Output
IEA	International Energy Agency
IMF	International Monetary Fund
IPA	investment promotion agency
IPCC	Intergovernmental Panel on Climate Change
JV	joint venture
M&As	mergers and acquisitions
MNE	multinational enterprise
MRIO	multiregional input-output model
OECD	Organisation for Economic Co-operation and Development
R&D	research and development
SDGs	Sustainable Development Goals
TCFD	Task Force on Climate-Related Financial Disclosure
UN	United Nations

UNCTAD	United Nations Conference on Trade and Development
WBCSD	World Business Council for Sustainable Development
WIDA	World Investment for Development Alliance
WRI	World Resources Institute
WTO	World Trade Organization

1. Introduction

This report considers the role of multinational enterprises (MNEs) in climate change, both as a fundamental risk and an opportunity for climate change mitigation. In many countries, a small number of MNEs influence a majority of greenhouse gas (GHG) emissions through their supply chains. Recent work from Climate Action 100+ considered the combined direct and indirect GHG emissions of companies, and found that 157 MNEs are responsible for over 60 percent of industrial carbon dioxide emissions. This means that the climate ambitions of MNEs will affect the environmental performance of countries around the world. As a leading actor, proactive MNEs could therefore impose sustainability standards or encourage green technology transfers within their supply chains that, in some cases, would affect millions of producers (Thorlakson, Zegher, and Lambin 2018) and accelerate the climate transition. However, obstructive MNEs may equally hold back any progress to reduce a country's emissions via inaction or even by actively resisting, obstructing, or lobbying against change.

Multinational enterprises also offer an important source of finance for sustainable development by supplying countries with foreign direct investment (FDI). Fulfilling the global commitments made in the Paris Agreement on climate change and achieving the Sustainable Development Goals (SDGs)[1] requires an acceleration in financing. The United Nations Conference on Trade and Development (UNCTAD 2014) estimates that between US$550 and US$850 billion in capital investment is needed in developing countries annually to meet goals related to climate mitigation, while another US$80 billion to US$120 billion is needed for adaptation. The United Nations (UN) estimated an average annual SDG funding gap of US$2.5 trillion in developing countries (UNEP 2018). Together with public and other private investments, the cross-border investments of MNEs (FDI) offer an important source of finance for sustainable development (OECD 2022).

This report builds on the research and key policy initiatives from several international organizations that have focused on the sustainable investment aspects of MNEs. This includes the Organisation for Economic Co-operation and Development's (OECD) *FDI Qualities Policy Toolkit*.[2] This initiative provides new insights into the ways FDI affects carbon emissions while offering policy recommendations to help governments attract FDI that contributes to decarbonization by reducing the emissions associated with foreign investments and inducing low-carbon spillovers to domestic firms (OECD 2022). UNCTAD's latest *World Investment Reports* have also included important new analyses on sustainable investment dynamics (UNCTAD 2021, 2022).

To encourage investment for sustainable development, the World Trade Organization's (WTO) investment facilitation agreement also makes explicit mention of the aim to expand and retain FDI flows to achieve sustainable development goals (WTO 2021). Other notable initiatives include a toolkit on investment facilitation for sustainable investment from the Columbia Center on Sustainable Investment (Berger, Kagan, and Sauvant 2021), and the World Investment for Development Alliance (WIDA), which is a new global platform dedicated to promoting investment for sustainable development.[3]

The objective of this report is to study the effect of MNEs on climate change. Toward this goal, the report reviews the latest available data, conducts new empirical analysis, and summarizes pioneering literature. Due to data limitations, previous work on MNEs and climate change has been relatively high-level in nature. Analysis has often focused on aggregate investment flows in the energy sector (for example, comparing the number of new greenfield FDI[4] project announcements in fossil fuels versus renewables) (OECD 2022) or investment in financial products related to the "environmental, social, and governance" (ESG) category (UNCTAD 2021, 2022). Little work has gone into directly observing the role that MNEs have on their global carbon emissions via their supply chains. Yet, this is a very active area of research, with new literature, datasets, and empirical analyses appearing more frequently in the last few years. This provides a good time to conduct a review of the latest available data and literature and illustrate their relevance for policy makers devising climate change mitigation strategies around the world. Each of the next four chapters aims to answer a separate question, utilizing a range of datasets and empirical approaches.

Chapter 2 asks what effect MNEs currently have on climate change. This starts by identifying three channels that shape MNEs' impact on climate change: the scale effect (emissions increases linked to MNE production), the technology effect (emissions reductions associated with diffusion of low-carbon knowledge and technology); and the composition effect (the ambiguous effect of MNEs on emissions as their FDI changes countries' industrial structure). Next, we consider the effect of MNEs on climate change by considering two types of data and empirical methods.

First, we consider bottom-up approaches that build estimates by collecting, processing, and aggregating firm-level data (see table 1.1). For this, we rely on the Full GHG Emissions Dataset from CDP (formerly the Carbon Disclosure Project) that provides emissions data for over 6,400 firms. However, not all firms in the database are analyzed, as it is currently not possible to identify the full ownership status of firms (and so, to distinguish the effect of MNEs). As an alternative, we focus analysis on 157 very large MNEs identified by Climate Action 100+, whose supply chains jointly make up most of the world's carbon emissions.[5] Next, to understand how the global supply chains of these firms affect each country's emissions targets, we exploit Bureau Van Dijk's Orbis database on MNEs' global affiliate structure and financial performance. We use this to apportion each MNE's global emissions based on its affiliates' relative financial performance within the MNE. Finally, to identify its global or country-level emissions shares, we then

TABLE 1.1 Key Datasets and Methodologies

Data	Key question	Methodology
CDP's (formerly the Carbon Disclosure Project) Full GHG (Greenhouse Gas) Emissions Dataset provides carbon emissions data for 6,400+ firms. Climate Action 100+ data identify 157 MNEs with the highest carbon emissions in the world and their overall climate commitments.	What effect do MNEs have on the emissions of their supply chains? (chapter 2)	• Identify 157 large MNEs from Climate Action 100+ and detect their global emissions using CDP's database. • Use Orbis data to identify the global ownership structure and financial information of 157 large MNEs to apportion global emissions across all their affiliates. • Estimate the global/country-level emissions share of 157 large MNEs by comparing their total emissions to OECD's Annual GHG Air Emissions Accounts.
Orbis provides ownership (including MNEs' global affiliate structure) and financial information for over 140 million firms. OECD Annual Air Emission and GHG Accounts. Accounts provides each country's total and sectoral carbon emissions.	How committed are leading MNEs to transitioning their supply chains to net-zero emissions by 2050? (chapter 4)	• Consider the overall commitment of 157 large MNEs using Climate Action 100+ data. • Use Orbis data to consider the global ownership structure of 157 large MNEs and thereby consider the climate commitments of all their affiliates. • Categorize countries based on emissions shares of affiliates of 157 large MNEs (using CDP, Orbis, and OECD), as well as climate commitments of affiliates of 157 large MNEs (using Climate Action 100+ and Orbis).
World Bank Enterprise Survey's Green Economy Module provides data on nine green firm characteristics for 36 countries (2018–20).	How do interactions with MNEs shape the potential of green technology transfers? (chapter 3)	• Regression analysis to consider how different interactions between domestic firms and MNEs (via investment, partnership, and trade) affect domestic firms' green technology transfers.

Sources: World Bank based on CDP, Climate Action 100+, OECD, and Orbis data.

Note: CDP = formerly the Carbon Disclosure Project; GHG = greenhouse gas; MNE = multinational enterprise; OECD = Organisation for Economic Co-operation and Development.

compare the MNE's global or affiliate emissions to country-level emissions from the Organisation for Economic Co-operation and Development's (OECD) Annual Air Emission and Greenhouse Gas (GHG) Accounts.

Second, we also consider top-down approaches to analyze carbon emissions from MNEs that start from macro-level emissions data at the country- or sector-level, and use a combination of trade, production, and investment data to apportion these emissions to MNEs and domestic firms. Using each approach, we will present new estimates from the latest available data and global literature to illustrate the size of each of these three channels in more detail.

Chapter 3 considers how countries can stimulate green technology transfers to domestic firms. For this question, the team analyzes the World Bank Enterprise Survey data in two regions (Europe and Central Asia and the Middle East and North Africa), which have a dedicated green module that considers firms' emissions monitoring, target setting, and specific actions to reduce carbon emissions. We use such data to conduct firm-level regression analysis and consider how three forms of partnerships with MNEs affect a company's environmental performance: equity partnerships with foreign firms, technological licensing from foreign-owned companies, and international supply links. This will provide some indication about the most appropriate policies to strengthen green technology transfers. We further use survey data to illustrate the important role that government policy plays in stimulating MNEs to invest in environmental activities and green technology transfers.

Chapter 4 then considers how committed leading MNEs currently are to decarbonizing their supply chains. Analysis for this question will start with the Climate Action 100+ database on 157 MNEs, which provides detailed information on each MNE's commitments to transition to net-zero emissions by 2050, and then consider the presence of any long-term, medium-term or short-term strategies toward decarbonization. To review the country-level commitment of MNEs, we again exploit Orbis and CDP to apportion each MNE's global emissions to their MNE affiliates (see table 1.1). We then consider the share of MNEs committed to a net-zero transition and weigh commitment based on their total emissions in the country.[6] We then consider the current weaknesses in corporate climate reporting and the presence of "greenwashing," in which companies intentionally give an overly flattering representation of their climate actions. Finally, we discuss the presence of specific market failures in corporate target setting, monitoring, and reporting.

Finally, Chapter 5 considers what types of policies can influence multinational enterprises' effect on climate. Here we introduce a new framework arguing that policy makers can use a range of policy tools (which we refer to as the 5Ps) to help MNEs mitigate their impact on climate change and better stimulate green growth. The 5Ps are patrolling (monitoring emissions), prescription (laws and regulations), penalties (taxes and charges), payments (incentives and fiscal support), and persuasion (corporate commitments and information). These tools can encourage MNEs to reduce their emissions-intensive production (scale), help MNEs shift their supply chains to lower-carbon production methods (technology), and facilitate a shift toward a low-carbon industrial structure by attracting green FDI and phasing out dirty sectors (composition). Each approach has several policy instruments to affect the scale, technology, and composition channels of MNE on climate change (table 5.1). This chapter then relies on a literature review to go through each of the 5Ps, illustrate which market failure or failures they seek to address, and elaborate on their advantages and disadvantages. Finally, we briefly discuss how policy makers can think about prioritizing and sequencing the 5Ps within a climate change mitigation strategy.

The report is widely targeted, such that the analysis and discussion is accessible to both policy researchers and policy makers. Chapters 2, 3, and 4 present assessment of estimation techniques and analysis of data using regression techniques and should be more relevant for researchers and analysts. The discussion of policy tools in chapter 5 should be relevant for both policy researchers and policy makers.

Notes

1. SDG Goal 13 is climate action and calls for urgent action to combat climate change and its impacts.
2. The FDI Qualities Policy Toolkit is designed to help governments identify priorities for policy reforms to strengthen FDI impacts in four SDG areas: productivity and innovation; job quality and skills; gender equality; and decarbonization.
3. See https://www.widalliance.org/ for more details.
4. Greenfield FDI refers to investments where a parent company establishes or expands a subsidiary in a foreign country—as opposed to mergers and acquisitions, which occur when a company purchases or leases an existing facility from another company.
5. For more details, see https://www.climateaction100.org/.
6. In this case, we assume that the emissions commitment of the MNE affiliate follows the ambitions set by the headquarters. However, going forward, it would also be important to monitor and review how host countries could shape the climate ambitions from MNE affiliates, to ensure they either match or exceed headquarters' targets.

References

Berger, Axel, Yardenne Kagan, and Karl P. Sauvant, eds. 2022. *Investment Facilitation for Development: A Toolkit for Policymakers,* 2nd ed. Geneva: International Trade Center (ITC). https://doi.org/10.2139/ssrn.3830031.

CDP (formerly the Carbon Disclosure Project). 2022. *CDP Full GHG Emissions Dataset 2022: Summary. CDP,* London. https://www.cdp.net/en/investor/ghg-emissions-dataset.

OECD (Organisation for Economic Co-operation and Development). 2022. *FDI Qualities Policy Toolkit.* Paris: OECD Publishing. https://doi.org/10.1787/7ba74100-en.

Thorlakson, T., J. F. de Zegher, and E. F. Lambin. 2018. "Companies' Contribution to Sustainability through Global Supply Chains." *Proceedings of the National Academy of Sciences* 115 (9): 2072–77. https://doi.org/10.1073/pnas.1716695115.

UNCTAD (United Nations Conference on Trade and Development). 2014. *World Investment Report 2014—Investing in the SDGs: An Action Plan.* Geneva: UNCTAD.

UNCTAD (United Nations Conference on Trade and Development). 2021. *World Investment Report 2021—Investing in Sustainable Recovery.* Geneva: UNCTAD.

UNCTAD (United Nations Conference on Trade and Development). 2022. *World Investment Report 2022—International Tax Reforms and Sustainable Investment.* Geneva: UNCTAD.

UNEP (United Nations Environment Programme). 2018. *Towards a Pollution-Free Planet: Background Report.* Nairobi: UNEP.

WTO (World Trade Organization). 2021. "Joint Statement on Investment Facilitation for Development." WT/L/1130, December 10, 2021. Geneva: WTO.

2. The Effect of Multinational Enterprises on Climate Change

Hypotheses and Channels

There are two main theories about the impact of foreign investors on the host country's environment: the pollution haven hypothesis and the pollution halo hypothesis. The pollution haven hypothesis states that firms with pollution-intensive processes move from high-income countries with stringent environmental regulations to developing countries with weaker environmental regulations. Consequently, developing countries become "pollution havens" where rich countries relocate environmentally hazardous industries. In contrast, the pollution halo hypothesis claims that firms from high-income countries may actually reduce a host country's pollution because their production relies on greener technologies, and the dissemination of these environment-friendly practices enhances the domestic firms' environmental performance.

While the empirical evidence on these two hypotheses is vast, it has led to inconclusive results. The validity of the pollution haven is tested and confirmed in country studies such as those by Tang and Tan (2015) and Shahbaz, Haouas, and Van Hoang (2019) for Vietnam; Koçak and Şarkgüneşi (2018) for Türkiye; and Solarin et al. (2017) for Ghana. Similarly, cross-country analyses such as Sapkota and Bastola (2017) for Latin American countries; Hanif et al. (2019) and Nasir, Huynh, and Huong (2019) for emerging Asian economies; Benzerrouk, Abid, and Sekrafi (2021) for developing countries; and Duan and Jiang (2021) for developed and developing countries provide support. Zhu et al. (2016) used quantile regressions to show that the effect of foreign direct investment (FDI) on carbon emissions is negative in the middle- and high-emissions countries of the Southeast Asian Nations (ASEAN). Similarly, Waqih et al. (2019) implement panel data techniques to compare the short- and long-run effect of FDI on emissions in the South Asian region and find no evidence of the pollution haven hypothesis in the long run. Furthermore, Adeel-Farooq, Riaz, and Ali (2021) show that FDI from developed countries improves the overall environmental performance of low- and middle-income countries, but FDI from developing countries harms the ecosystems of low- and middle-income host countries. The authors suggest that the effect of FDI on the host country's pollution depends on the source country's environmental policy rather than the host country's environmental regulation.

Perhaps the main reason for the inconclusive results between the pollution haven/halo theories is that this binary view is too simplistic. The mixed conclusions above arise from several factors, such as the methodology implemented by the authors, the country or group of countries studied, and the period of analysis. More crucially, however, is that they aggregate multinational enterprises' (MNE) effect as increasing or reducing carbon emissions. Yet, MNEs and FDI can simultaneously bring with them challenges and opportunities for climate change mitigation through three key channels (OECD 2022):

- **Scale effect:** MNEs are major drivers of emissions. As they increase their production, the country would likely also increase its total emissions.
- **Technology effect**: MNEs can help diffuse low-carbon knowledge and technology to domestic firms, which can thereby reduce a sector's average carbon intensity and reduce emissions.
- **Composition effect:** MNEs' FDI also changes the industrial structure. This has an ambiguous effect on emissions, as such FDI could help shift resources toward low- or high-carbon intensity activities.

The rest of this chapter looks at the effect of MNEs on emissions in more detail, by considering two types of data and empirical methods: bottom-up (firm-level) and top-down (macro-level) approaches. Using each approach, we present new estimates from the latest available data and global literature to illustrate the size of each of these three channels in more detail.

Bottom-Up Approaches to Estimate the Effect of MNEs on Carbon Emissions

Methodology

Bottom-up approaches to analyzing carbon emissions build up estimates by collecting, processing, and aggregating firm-level data. Gathering firm-level data on emissions is challenging because accounting procedures can differ from establishment to establishment. Furthermore, the consolidation of sectoral-level estimates mainly depends on the homogeneity of the firms' reports in the sample. Nevertheless, bottom-up estimates can provide significant insights into the specific source of emissions and guide discussion and actions to alleviate the environmental impact.

The Greenhouse Gas Protocol Corporate Standard, a joint initiative by the World Resources Institute (WRI) and the World Business Council for Sustainable Development (WBCSD), classifies a firm's greenhouse gas (GHG) emissions into three scopes (figure 2.1; WRI and WBCSD 2004):

- **Scope 1 emissions** are direct emissions from owned or controlled sources. Direct GHG emissions are principally the result of activities such as generating electricity, heat, or steam; physical or chemical processing; transportation of materials,

FIGURE 2.1 Emissions Associated with Firms' Activities within Scope 1, 2, and 3

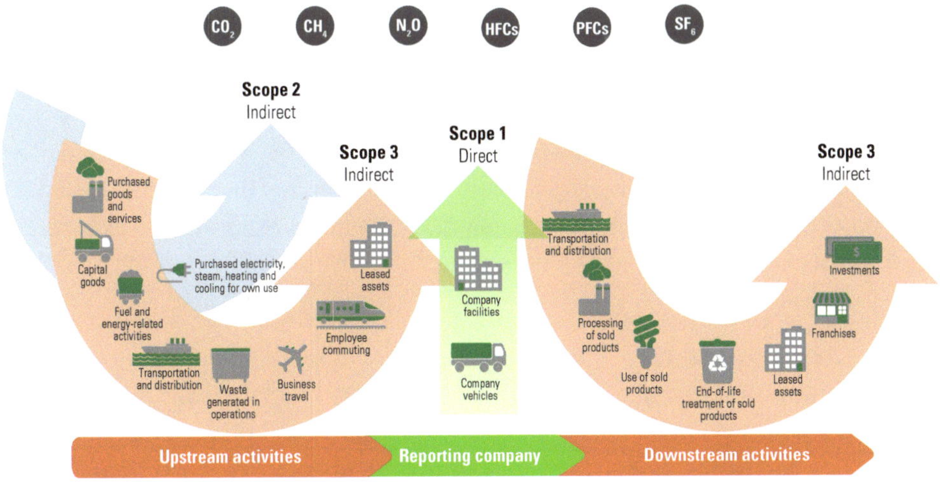

Source: WRI/WBCSD Corporate Value Chain (scope 3) Accounting and Reporting Standard (WRI and WBCSD 2004).

Note: WBCSD = World Business Council for Sustainable Development; WRI = World Resources Institute. CO_2 = Carbon dioxide; CH_4 = Methane; HFCs = Hydrofluorocarbons; N_2O = Nitrous oxide; PFCs = Perfluorocarbons; SF_6 = Sulfur hexafluoride.

products, waste, and employees; and fugitive emissions such as equipment leaks from joints, seals, packing, and gaskets.

- **Scope 2 emissions** are indirect emissions from the generation of purchased electricity, steam, heating, and cooling consumed by the firm.
- **Scope 3 emissions** are all indirect emissions (not included in scope 2) that occur in the firm's value chain. These include *upstream* emissions, which relate to the purchase and use of goods, services, energy, and capital in the production process. They also include *downstream* emissions, which mostly relate to the transport, processing, use, and disposal of sold products. This also includes emissions from services such as leased assets, franchises, and investments.

While there have been attempts to produce firm-level carbon estimates, challenges often emerge when reporting completeness, consistency, and accuracy. The literature on bottom-up carbon estimates originated from Heede (2014), who was first to analyze firms—rather than states—as the source of emissions. This started from a relatively crude approximation building on publicly available company reports filed with the US Securities and Exchange Commission on two emitting activities: fossil fuel and cement production. The carbon content was estimated using international averages of state-level emission reporting from the Intergovernmental Panel on Climate Change (IPCC) *Guidelines for National GHG Inventories* (Eggleston et al. 2006) While seminal, the study's methodology faced several challenges. First, reporting was partial, leaving out potentially important firms. Second, there was no agreed-upon standard for reporting emissions, potentially leading to inconsistent estimates. Third, the study was unable to account for heterogeneity in firm-level emissions across production (relying on global averages), thus limiting accuracy.

A new global dataset to estimate firm-level emissions comes from CDP's (formerly the Carbon Disclosure Project) Full GHG (Greenhouse Gas) Emissions Dataset, which solves most of the challenges. CDP works with companies to develop their emissions reporting. In return, it incorporates their emissions in a global database, which is also used to produce emissions estimates for companies that do not disclose. In addition, it relies on a global emissions reporting standard, and conducts extensive checks to verify accuracy (see box 2.1).

However, one major challenge remains for bottom-up approaches: double counting of scope 3 emissions. While recent advances in data collection have improved firm-level emission estimates, the bottom-up approach still lacks a systematic methodology for aggregating emissions. When multiple firms in the same value chain all calculate their scope 3 emissions, summation would lead to double counting and overestimate emissions. Yet, aggregating only scope 1 and 2 emissions tends to exclude essential activities within the supply chain and thus underestimate emissions. As such, aggregated estimates (including ours below) should be interpreted with caution. The ability to avoid double counting within supply chains is a clear advantage of top-down approaches (see "Scale" below).

The next few sections present some preliminary findings to consider the scale, technology, and composition effects of MNEs on climate change using bottom-up approaches. Much of this analysis makes use of CDP's database. However, not all firms in the database are analyzed, as it is currently not possible to identify the full ownership status of each of the 6,400 firms included in the database (and so, to distinguish the effect of MNEs). As an alternative, the choice was made to focus analysis on a small number of very large MNEs that emit most of the world's carbon emissions and focus in on their supply chain (scope 3) emissions. For this, we follow the Climate Action 100+, which identified 157 MNEs that have the highest combined direct and indirect GHG emissions in the world according to CDP data.[1] This analysis also serves as a proof-of-concept that could be extended to a larger set of firms (global or country-specific), going forward.

Scale

A small number of large MNEs account for the majority of global industrial CO_2 emissions (figure 2.2). In most countries, carbon emissions are heavily concentrated within a narrow set of firms. In Morocco, for example, the audit results of an energy efficiency training program for large corporations showed that 5 percent of the 8,000 companies accounted for 70 percent of industrial energy consumption (OECD 2022). A similar finding exists at the global level. The total emissions of 157 large MNEs jointly account

BOX 2.1 Methodology for Bottom-Up Approach to Analyzing Emissions: CDP's Full GHG Emissions Dataset

The most extensive and advanced global source of firm-level carbon emissions comes from the Full GHG Emissions Dataset owned and controlled by CDP, a global nonprofit. CDP works with companies, investors, cities, states, and regions. Firms collaborate with CDP to help them to accurately map their emissions, uncover risks and opportunities for carbon reduction, and track and benchmark progress. In return, their emissions data are incorporated in CDP's global database. CDP further uses these publicly disclosed figures to produce emissions estimates for companies that do not disclose. It also provides the means to improve the quality of company disclosures by identifying anomalies and engaging with the companies to resolve them. The full dataset includes data or estimates for over 6,400 companies. The sample consists of companies in the Morgan Stanley Capital International All-Country World Index (ACWI), as well as the highest emitting companies not included in this index.

Firm-Level Emissions Reporting

CDP's disclosure platform builds on the recommendations from the 2017 Task Force on Climate-Related Financial Disclosures (TCFD), which is increasingly recognized as the global standard for emission reporting. It translates these TCFD recommendations and pillars into disclosure questions and a standardized annual format. This leads to a detailed survey, which participating firms fill out every year.

CDP then conducts consistency checks for every company to verify that each data point aligns with other information that companies report internally (for example, ensuring consistency between reported energy use and scope 2 emissions) or externally (from other data sources). Large outliers are investigated in detail by reviewing companies' survey responses, and potentially removed. If a data point appears to be misreported, and the company is one of the top 200 highest emitters from the previous year, they are contacted for clarification. For missing or possibly misreported data, an estimate is provided alongside the reported value.

Modeling

To estimate the emissions for nonreporting firms, CDP uses various economic models. First, bottom-up modeling combines physical activity indicators (metric tons, barrels, kilometers, and so forth) with their associated emission factors. CDP's database relies on bottom-up models to estimate emissions across six homogeneous sectors: coal mining, oil and gas extraction, petroleum refining, electric power generation, steel production, and cement production. Second, in case a company has provided some but not all of the data points, CDP adopts a set of intra-company models that use the available data to calculate the remaining emissions and energy figures. Third, multivariate regression models are used to estimate emissions for sectors without bottom-up estimates, using company revenue and activity classification as predictor variables.

Source: World Bank adjusted calculations based on CDP (2020).

Note: GHG = greenhouse gas.

FIGURE 2.2 Global Industrial Emissions of the Supply Chains of Large MNEs, 2021

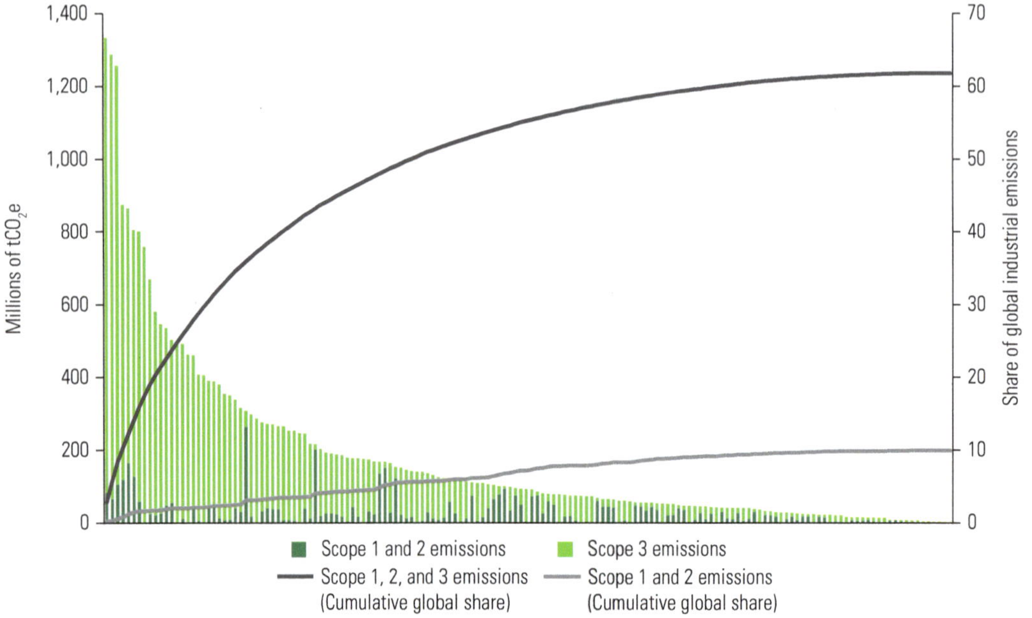

Sources: World Bank calculations based on CDP 2022a and OECD 2023.

Note: A total of 157 companies are identified based on Climate Action 100+. Each bar represents one MNE, while the lines provide their own emissions as cumulative shares of global industrial emissions. CDP = formerly the Carbon Disclosure Project; CO_2e = carbon dioxide equivalent; GHG = greenhouse gas; MNE = multinational enterprise; OECD = Organisation for Economic Co-operation and Development; t = tons of CO_2.

for up to 60 percent of total industrial emissions.[2] Their own activities (scope 1 and 2) jointly account for (only) 10 percent of global industrial emissions. The largest share of emissions from these MNEs pertains to their supply chain (scope 3), which may make up to 50 percent of global emissions.

Most of the 157 large MNEs are headquartered in Europe, North America, and Asia, and around half of the sample is in the energy industry. Table 2.1 illustrates the regional distribution of the 157 MNEs. This shows that these large emitting MNEs are headquartered mostly in Europe (56 firms), North America (52 firms), and Asia (32 firms). These 157 large MNEs are active in four broad sectors: energy, industrials, transportation, and consumer goods and services. Around half the group is based in energy (75 firms), heavily concentrated in the oil and gas and electricity utilities subsectors. Other sectors are industrials (45 firms), transportation (25 firms), and consumer goods and services (12 firms).

The energy sector is the biggest source of industrial emissions from 157 large MNEs, followed by the industrial sector (figure 2.3). The joint emissions from the activities of MNEs and their supply chains (scope 1, 2, and 3) make up the largest share of global industrial emissions in the energy sector (38 percent), led by oil and gas (26 percent), utilities (6 percent), and coal mining (4 percent). The industrial sector follows, with large MNEs accounting for 15 percent of global emissions. MNEs in the transportation

TABLE 2.1 Regional Distribution of 157 Large MNEs and Their Share of Global Emissions

		Number of firms by region of headquarters						
Sector	**Subsector**	**Africa**	**Asia**	**Europe**	**North America**	**Oceania**	**South America**	**Total**
Energy	Coal mining	0	4	0	0	0	0	4
	Electricity utilities	1	3	12	13	1	0	30
	Oil and gas	1	9	10	11	3	2	36
	Oil and gas distribution	0	0	2	3	0	0	5
	Total	2	16	24	27	4	2	75
Industrials	Cement	1	1	3	2	2	0	9
	Chemicals	0	1	4	1	0	0	6
	Diversified mining	0	1	4	1	2	1	9
	Other industrials	0	4	4	4	0	0	12
	Paper	0	0	0	1	0	1	2
	Steel	0	3	4	0	0	0	7
	Total	1	10	19	9	4	2	45
Transportation	Airlines	0	0	1	3	1	0	5
	Autos	0	5	5	2	0	0	12
	Other transport	0	0	3	4	0	0	7
	Shipping	0	0	1	0	0	0	1
	Total	0	5	10	9	1	0	25
Consumer goods and services		0	1	3	7	1	0	12
Grand total		**3**	**32**	**56**	**52**	**10**	**4**	**157**

Source: World Bank calculations using CDP's database.

Note: CDP = formerly Carbon Disclosure Project; GHG = greenhouse gas; MNE = multinational enterprise. 157 companies are identified based on Climate Action 100+.

sector jointly make up 7 percent of global emissions, and finally the MNEs in consumer goods and services sector account for 2 percent of global emissions.

Once we consider the supply chains of the 157 large MNEs, their global emissions significantly outweigh their global share in economic output. To put the activities of these MNEs in perspective, figure 2.4 contrasts the MNEs' share of global emissions by sector with their share in global gross domestic product (GDP; using MNEs' annual reported global turnover). When considering only the emissions from their own activities (panel a), the emissions from firms outweigh the global shares in economic output for a few sectors (those to the upper-left side of the 45-degree line). These include the oil and gas and electricity utilities sectors (both represented in the top-right corner as outliers), as well as steel, cement, and chemicals. Yet, when the carbon emissions from supply chains (panel b) are also included, almost all these sectors' emissions significantly outweigh their global shares in economic output. This is most extremely visible in the case of oil and gas, with MNEs' direct sales accounting for only 3.5 percent of GDP but 26 percent of global emissions.

FIGURE 2.3 Global Share of Industrial Emissions from 157 Large MNEs, by Sector, 2021

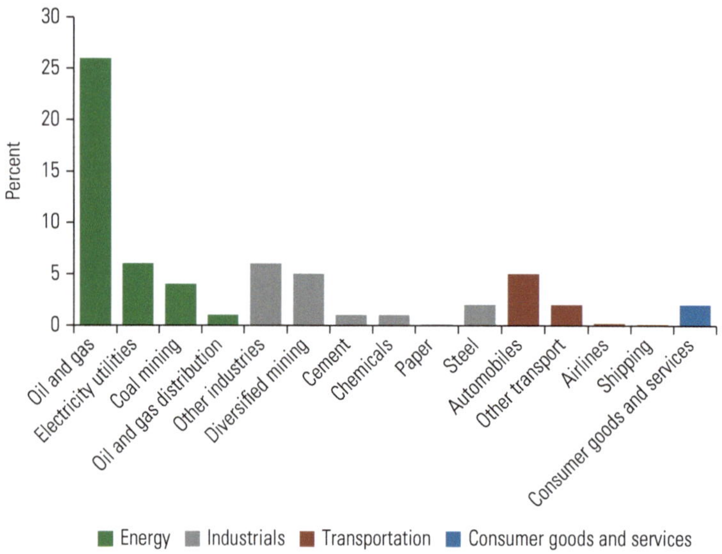

Sources: World Bank calculations using CDP 2022a and OECD 2023.

Note: A total of 157 companies are identified based on Climate Action 100+. CDP = formerly the Carbon Disclosure Project; GHG = greenhouse gas; MNE = multinational enterprise; OECD = Organisation for Economic Co-operation and Development.

FIGURE 2.4 Global Share of Industrial Emissions and GDP from 157 Large MNEs, by Sector, 2021

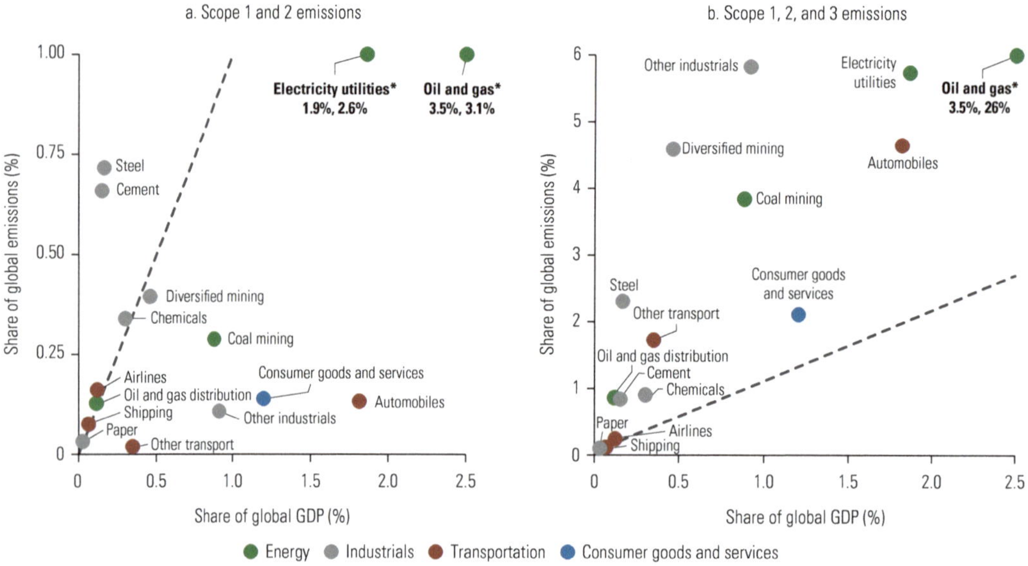

Sources: World Bank calculations based on CDP, Orbis, and WDI GDP data.

Note: A total of 157 companies are identified based on Climate Action 100+. The gray bars represent the 45-degree line with equal emissions-GDP weight. Scope 1 emissions are direct emissions from owned or controlled sources. Scope 2 emissions are indirect emissions from the generation of purchased electricity, steam, heating, and cooling consumed by the firm. Scope 3 emissions are all indirect emissions (not included in scope 2) that occur in the firm's value chain. Extreme outliers are bolded and marked with an asterisk (*). CDP = formerly the Carbon Disclosure Project; GDP = gross domestic product; GHG = greenhouse gas; MNE = multinational enterprise. WDI = World Development Indicators.

The type of scope 3 emissions of these 157 large MNEs differs considerably by sector (figure 2.5). In the case of the energy and mining sectors, most emissions are associated with the downstream use of product—for example, 98 percent for coal mining, 95 percent for diversified mining, and 93 percent for oil and gas. In contrast, sectors that utilize significant energy in production see most of their emissions in upstream activities—for example, 93 percent for airlines, 89 percent for shipping and cement, and 71 percent for chemicals. In some cases, they may be more balanced—such as for consumer goods and services (48 percent upstream, 52 percent downstream). Overall, the bulk of total emissions lies in the downstream use, covering 85 percent of all the 157 MNEs' scope 3 emissions.

To further understand the emissions impact of these 157 MNEs requires reviewing the structure of their global affiliates. Most companies only report their own global emissions. Yet, to understand how the supply chains of these firms affect each country's emissions targets, it is important to apportion such global scope 1, 2, and 3 emissions by country. This report has made an initial attempt to do so using data from Bureau Van Dijk's Orbis database, which provides data on MNEs' global activities based on their affiliates' location, revenue, total assets, and employment numbers. We use this information to apportion emissions associated with the

FIGURE 2.5 Breakdown of Scope 3 Emissions of 157 Large MNEs, by Sector, 2021

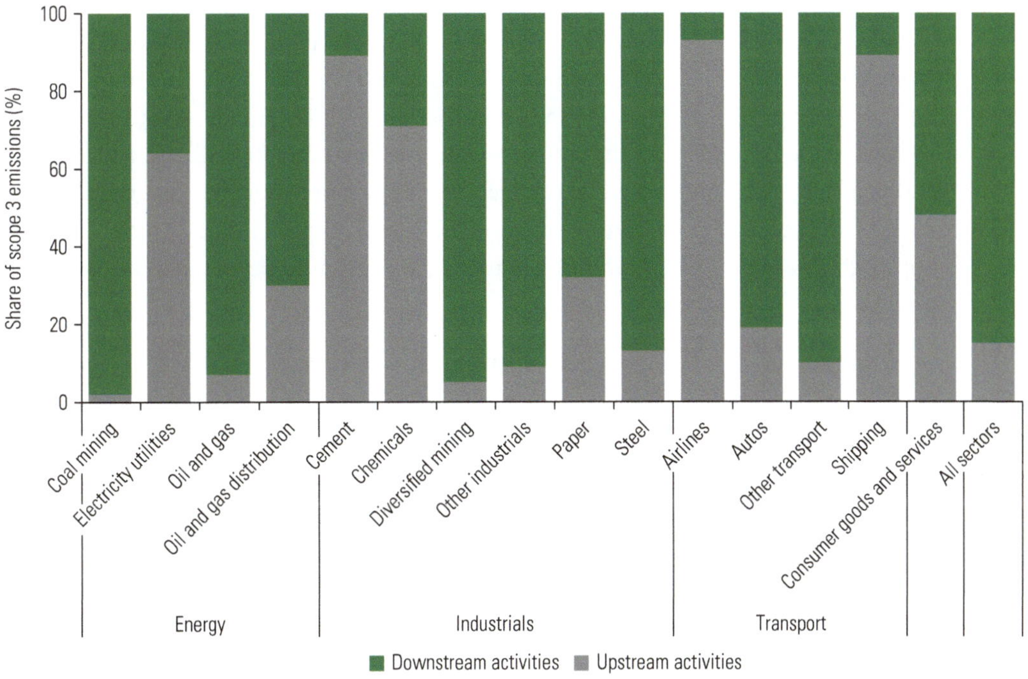

Source: World Bank calculations using CDP database.

Note: A total of 157 companies are identified based on Climate Action 100+. Scope 3 emissions are all indirect emissions (not included in scope 2) that occur in the firm's value chain. CDP = formerly the Carbon Disclosure Project; GHG = greenhouse gas; MNE = multinational enterprise.

various types of activities related to their scope 1, 2, and 3 emissions based on each affiliate's relative share within the MNE. For example, scope 3 emissions associated with capital goods are apportioned proportionate to each affiliate's relative share of assets, while scope 3 emissions associated with employee commuting is apportioned proportionate to the affiliate's relative share of employment. The full detailed methodology used for apportioning global emissions to MNE affiliates is provided in annex 2A.

A breakdown by country shows the global reach and concentration of emissions associated with the activities of these 157 MNEs. Map 2.1 tries to apportion the global scope 1, 2, and 3 emissions for the 157 large MNEs to country-level estimates based on affiliate activities (see above and annex 2A). It then compares these to each country's annual emissions. This illustrates, first, that these 157 MNEs have an extremely global reach. Out of the 181 countries in the world that reported GDP figures in 2021, they had active affiliates in 136 (75 percent), and these countries make up 99.3 percent of global GDP. When considering the emissions from their direct activities (panel a), we see that these MNEs accounted for 1–25 percent of emissions in 85 countries, another 25–50 percent in 9 countries (in Australia, Chile, Europe, and South Africa) and upwards of 50 percent in 13 countries (all in Europe).

We also consider the overall emissions from MNEs, including their supply chains (panel b). This shows that these 157 MNEs further accounted for less than 25 percent of emissions across 85 countries (largely concentrated in Africa and Latin America). They made up 25–50 percent in 9 countries (most notably China, Mexico, and the United States), 50–75 percent in another 8 countries (notably Brazil, Colombia, India, and Poland), and 75–100 percent in 9 countries (including Canada, Italy, the Russian Federation, and Thailand). Then, for 25 countries the emissions accounted for over 100 percent of their emissions—this largely relates to those countries that headquarter such MNEs in Australia, South Africa, and Western Europe.[3] As such, this bottom-up approach showcases the significant geographic concentration of emissions associated with the activities of these 157 MNEs.

A breakdown by MNE affiliates also shows that countries differ significantly in sectors with the biggest emissions. Map 2.2 summarizes the biggest emissions associated with the affiliate activities of the 157 large MNEs. This shows the wide variety across countries. The biggest share tends to come from energy sectors. Over 60 countries have oil and gas production as their main emission source, 11 countries' emissions are dominated by electricity utility companies, while for 2 countries (India and Indonesia) the main emission source is coal mining. Interestingly, alongside oil and gas, the African continent tends to dominate based on industrials; most notably cement, diversified mining, other industrials, and steel. A select number of countries dominate in transport such as autos (including Germany and Japan), and other transport (Saudi Arabia). Consumer goods and services are the dominant source of emissions for

MAP 2.1 Share of Country-Level Emissions Associated with the Affiliate Activities of 157 Large MNEs, 2021

a. Scope 1 and 2 emissions

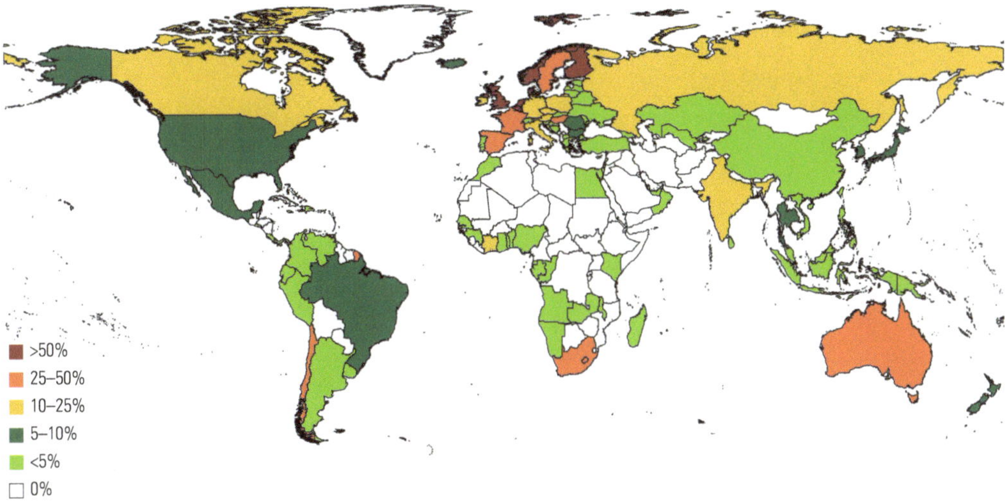

b. Scope 1, 2, and 3 emissions

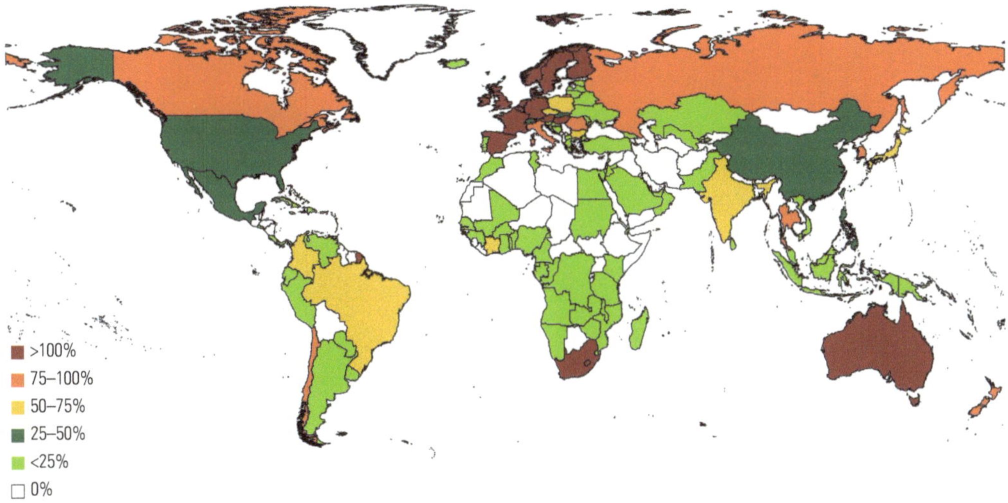

Sources: World Bank calculations using CDP, Climate Action 100+, OECD, and Orbis data.

Note: The 157 companies are identified based on Climate Action 100+. Firms' production and supply chain–based emissions are compared to country-level reported consumption-based emissions. Because countries may partly export their carbon-intensive production abroad, MNE-based emissions can account for over 100 percent of country-reported emissions. Scope 1 emissions are direct emissions from owned or controlled sources. Scope 2 emissions are indirect emissions from the generation of purchased electricity, steam, heating, and cooling consumed by the firm. Scope 3 emissions are all indirect emissions (not included in scope 2) that occur in the firm's value chain. CDP = formerly the Carbon Disclosure Project; GDP = gross domestic product; GHG = greenhouse gas; MNE = multinational enterprise; OECD = Organisation for Economic Co-operation and Development.

MAP 2.2 Sectors with the Biggest Emissions Associated with Affiliate Activities of 157 Large MNEs, 2021

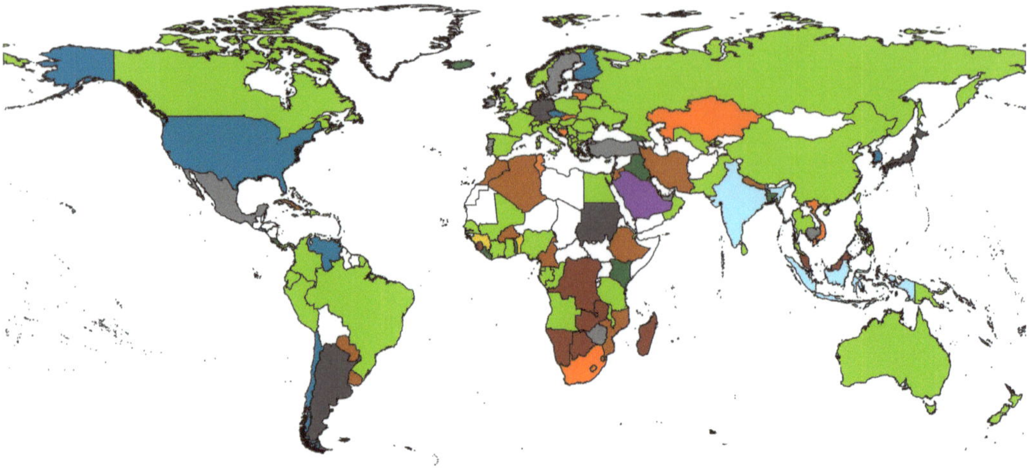

Sources: World Bank calculations based on World Bank calculations using CDP, OECD, and Orbis data.

Note: 157 companies are identified based on Climate Action 100+. CDP = formerly the Carbon Disclosure Project; GHG = greenhouse gas; MNE = multinational enterprise; OECD = Organisation for Economic Co-operation and Development.

another 15 countries (mostly in Africa, Latin America, and the Middle East). The difference in MNEs' sectoral make-up across countries is further illustrated in box 2.2, which provides country examples for India and South Africa.

Technology

The bottom-up approach also has some potential for exploring the technology effect associated with MNEs. Anecdotal findings often support the hypothesis that MNEs use less carbon-intensive production methods than domestic firms. For example, Chevron, a large MNE energy company, has significantly changed its oil production methods to reduce methane emissions (an extremely potent greenhouse gas). By making changes to their air compressors and tank vents, and by shifting away from pneumatic controls, Chevron was able to reduce methane emissions to less than a fifth of the industry average (*Economist* 2022). Evidence increasingly suggests that MNEs can diffuse low-carbon knowledge and technology to domestic firms, which can thereby reduce a sector's average carbon intensity, and reduce emissions (Adeel-Farooq, Riaz, and Ali 2021).

New evidence confirms that MNEs are considerably less carbon intensive in the production of steel and cement. Data from CDP's firm surveys (corporate response data) provide evidence to support the potential for MNEs to reduce a country's

BOX 2.2 Select Country Examples—the Emissions of Large MNEs in India and South Africa

India

Out of the 157 large multinational enterprises (MNEs), 5 are headquartered in India (in the mining, oil and gas, and electricity utilities subsectors). However, a total of 77 of the large MNEs have at least one affiliate in India. This leads to a total of 977 MNE affiliates in our database. A more detailed breakdown of their numbers, relative economic weight, and share of India's emissions is given in table B2.2.1. This first shows the extreme significance of India's coal mining for MNE emissions. The output of the 159 coal-mining MNE affiliates only account for 0.4 percent of India's gross domestic product (GDP), but because of the significant emissions associated with burning coal, this together would account for almost 36 percent of India's reported emissions. The second-largest emissions come from the oil and gas industry, whose MNE affiliates account for around 2.6 percent of GDP, but 16 percent of emissions. The third biggest emissions come from the category "Other industrials," which includes production of machinery and electrical and electronic equipment, and jointly accounts for 0.8 percent of GDP and 3.3 percent of the country's reported emissions.

TABLE B2.2.1 The Effect of Large MNEs' Affiliates on India's Carbon Emissions, 2021

Sector	Subsector	# of MNE affiliates	Share of GDP (%)	Share of country's reported emissions (%)	
				Scope 1 and 2	Scope 1, 2, and 3
Energy	Coal mining	159	0.4	1.9	35.8
	Electricity utilities	175	0.5	7.4	8.6
	Oil and gas	386	2.6	2.2	16.2
	Oil and gas distribution	1	0.0	0.0	0.0
	Total	**721**	**3.5**	**11.4**	**60.5**
Industrials	Cement	9	0.2	0.3	0.4
	Chemicals	23	0.1	0.0	0.0
	Diversified mining	30	0.3	0.7	1.0
	Other industrials	77	0.8	0.0	3.3
	Steel	23	0.1	0.1	0.4
	Total	**153**	**1.2**	**0.9**	**4.8**
Transportation	Airlines	1	0.0	0.0	0.0
	Autos	37	1.5	0.1	2.7
	Other transport	8	0.1	0.0	0.2
	Shipping	3	0.0	0.0	0.0
	Total	**49**	**1.6**	**0.1**	**2.9**
Consumer goods and services		45	1.1	0.0	0.8
Overall total		**977**	**7.7**	**12.7**	**69.4**

(Box continues on the following page.)

BOX 2.2. Select Country Examples—the Emissions of Large MNEs in India and South Africa (continued)

South Africa

Out of the 157 large MNEs in our dataset, 2 are headquartered in South Africa (in the oil and gas and electricity utilities subsectors). Yet, a total of 48 of the large MNEs have at least one affiliate in South Africa. In total, we identified 138 MNE affiliates active in this country. Table B2.2.2 provides a more detailed breakdown. This shows, first, that there are 7 MNE affiliates that are active in steel production, whose output makes up around 4 percent of South Africa's GDP, and their supply chain's overall emissions amount to almost half of South Africa's reported carbon emissions. The second- and third-largest emissions are from its electricity utilities and oil and gas companies, accounting for 3 percent of GDP each, but making up 37 and 18 percent of the country's reported emissions, respectively.

TABLE B2.2.2 The Effect of Large MNEs' Affiliates on South Africa's Carbon Emissions, 2021

Sector	Subsector	# of MNE affiliates	Share of GDP (%)	Share of country's reported emissions (%)	
				Scope 1 and 2	Scope 1, 2, and 3
Energy	Electricity utilities	27	3.4	34.8	37.1
	Oil and gas	20	3.5	11.2	17.7
	Total	47	6.9	45.9	54.8
Industrials	Cement	3	0.4	0.1	0.2
	Chemicals	12	10.3	1.9	9.1
	Diversified mining	20	2.5	0.2	5.3
	Other industrials	16	1.9	0.1	2.4
	Steel	7	4.4	0.5	49.0
	Total	58	19.4	2.8	66.0
Transportation	Autos	17	6.2	0.1	5.7
	Other transport	2	0.1	0.0	0.1
	Total	19	6.3	0.1	5.8
Consumer goods and services		14	2.8	0.4	4.0
Overall total		138	35.4	49.2	130.6

Source: World Bank calculations using CDP, Climate Action 100+, OECD, and Orbis data.

Table Note: Firms' production and supply chain–based emissions are compared to country-level reported consumption-based emissions. CDP = formerly the Carbon Disclosure Project; GDP = gross domestic product; GHG = greenhouse gas; MNE = multinational enterprise; OECD = Organisation for Economic Co-operation and Development.

emissions via their technology. Figure 2.6 considers the carbon intensity of production of two products: steel and cement, and compares the performance of domestic firms versus MNEs. Panel a shows that in the case of steel, MNEs considerably overperform vis-à-vis domestic firms using blast furnaces (producing 25 percent fewer emissions for the same output), direct reduced iron electric arc furnaces (producing 48 percent fewer emissions), and scrap-electric arc furnaces (producing 18 percent fewer emissions).[4]

Panel b shows that for cement, the results differ more significantly across product types. For clinkers, emissions intensity is roughly similar, while for cement equivalent and cementitious products, MNEs were able to produce the same goods for somewhere between 6 to 11 percent fewer emissions. Yet, in the case of low-CO_2 material,[5] the average MNE was found to produce goods with 84 percent fewer emissions than domestic firms.[6] Hence, while MNEs generally have a reduced carbon intensity of production in steel, for cement their advantage comes from the use of more sophisticated low-CO_2 products.[7] All in all, this does suggest that the dissemination of production technologies used by MNEs would have significant potential to reduce the emissions of domestic firms.

FIGURE 2.6 Carbon Intensity of Production, Domestic Firms versus MNEs, 2021

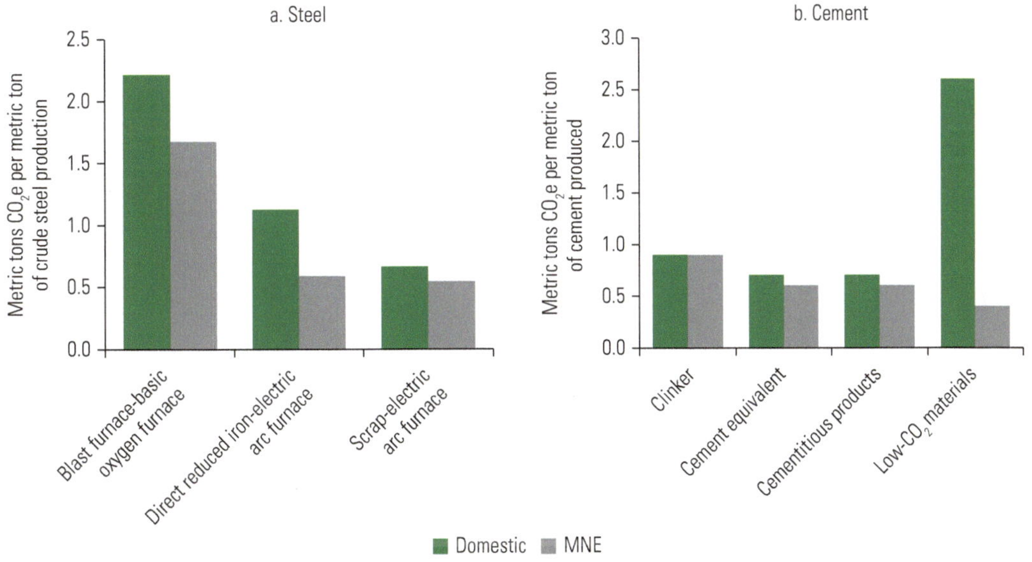

Source: World Bank estimates based on CDP Corporate Response Data.

Note: Figures on steel production are based on 28 companies—14 MNEs and 14 domestic firms. Figures on cement production are based on 24 companies—14 MNEs and 10 domestic firms. Each firm's ownership characteristics (foreign or domestic) were manually identified using the Bureau Van Dijk's Orbis database. Also see table 2A.2 and table 2A.3 in annex 2A for regression analysis exploring the effect of MNEs on the carbon intensity of production of steel and cement. CDP = formerly the Carbon Disclosure Project; CO_2e = carbon dioxide equivalent; MNE = multinational enterprise.

Composition

Finally, to evaluate the composition effect of MNEs, we evaluate FDI project announcements using a dedicated sectoral classification of green versus polluting sectors. To inform the shifting effect of MNEs' overseas investment on industrial structures around the world, we aggregate FDI announcements that are made around the world and consider whether these are more or less carbon intensive. To do this, we use data on greenfield FDI announcements (from FDI markets) and international mergers and acquisitions (using Refinitiv data). For each, we develop a dedicated sectoral classification that follows the European Union (EU) taxonomy for Sustainable Activities (European Commission 2020) to identify a set of green sectors (that accelerate a net-zero emissions future) and polluting sectors (that are inconsistent with a net-zero emissions future). Examples of green activities in the EU taxonomy include electricity generation from renewable energy, afforestation, and manufacturing of products that help the transition to a low-carbon economy (such as batteries and electronic vehicles) or which use low-CO_2 technology to produce traditionally high-CO_2 products (like steel and cement). Low-carbon transport activities (such as public rail) are also included. Finally, the EU taxonomy also includes some activities that have a broader environmental purpose such as water supply, sewerage, waste management, and remediation. Polluting activities are mostly confined to high-CO_2 mining or processing of fossil fuels; metals and minerals; and the conventional manufacturing of chemical, metal, and plastic products.

There appears to be a robust trend of FDI shifting out of polluting sectors and into green sectors (figure 2.7). Panel a shows that greenfield FDI announcements for polluting sectors have gradually declined. In contrast, FDI is increasingly pouring into green sectors, and since 2019 has overtaken polluting sectors. Panel b shows that for international mergers and acquisitions (M&As), the dynamics differed, with a growing number of announcements in polluting sectors until the mid-2010s. Since then, there has been a significant decline, and so the trendline follows an inverted U-curve. Firms in green sectors did see a substantial rise in announcements over time, so that in 2021 the value of green sector M&As overtook that of polluting sectors.

Global firms may be increasing their investments in sustainability for three main reasons. First, foreign investors are likely reacting to rapidly declining costs and significant growth potential in renewable energy generation and low-carbon manufacturing methods (IRENA 2020). Second, companies are also responding to the rising pressures brought upon them by governments and investors and shareholders to engage in lower-carbon activities. Some evidence of this is found in survey evidence summarized in "The Importance of Government Policy to Stimulate MNEs' Green Technology Transfers" in chapter 3 and figure 3.5. Third, companies are also responding to rising costs associated with polluting activities. Shareholders are increasingly pricing in a carbon risk premium at the firm level, which increases the cost of capital and means both a lower projected

FIGURE 2.7 Green versus Polluting Global FDI Announcements, 2001–21

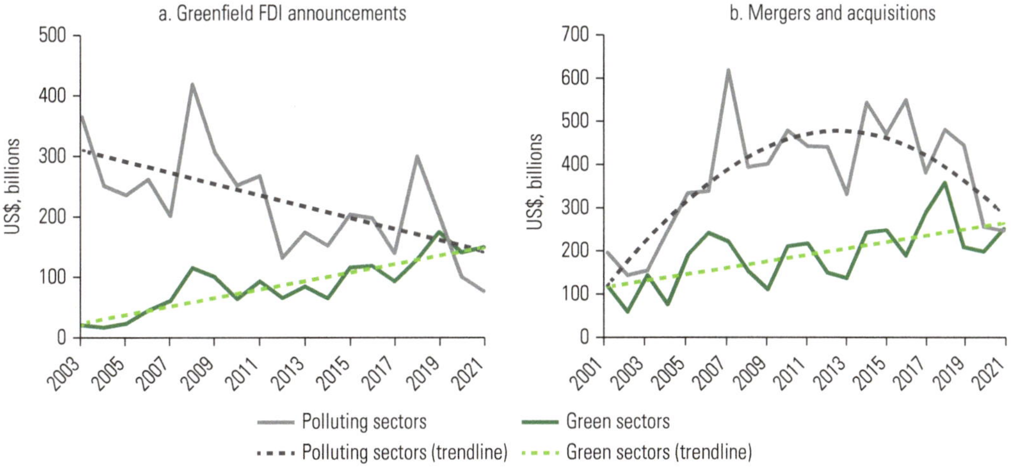

Sources: World Bank estimates based on FDI markets and Refinitiv data.

Note: Sectors classified in accordance with EU Taxonomy for Sustainable Activities. EU = European Union; FDI = foreign direct investment.

earnings stream and higher hurdle rates on new investment (Chava 2014). Bolton and Kacperczyk (2022) further find that while no carbon risk premium was identified in the 1990s, strong evidence of such rising costs was found in a 2017 sample period. Jointly, this explains a growing number of green and slowing number of polluting greenfield FDI and cross-border M&A announcements over time.

Top-Down Approaches to Estimate the Effect of MNEs on Carbon Emissions

Methodology

Top-down approaches to analyzing carbon emissions from MNEs start from macro-level emissions data at the country- and sector-level, and use a combination of trade, production, and investment data to apportion these emissions to MNEs and domestic firms. Examples of this approach can be found in Zhang et al. (2020), Borga et al. (2022), and Zhu, Guo, and Zhang (2022). In each case, the authors propose a framework to calculate the effect of MNEs' supply chains on carbon emissions by linking a carbon intensity matrix at the country-industry level with the multiregional input-output model (MRIO), an extension of the standard input-output matrix with independent rows and columns for each industry in each country (see box 2.3 for details).

The top-down approach allows researchers to avoid double-counting emissions and to utilize a standard framework for trade-related analysis. Using MRIO provides a systematic methodology to account for firms' carbon emissions that avoids the problems of double counting still present within bottom-up approaches. MRIO tables such as the Activities of Multinational Enterprises (AMNE) database[8] also allow performing calculations for several countries and industries under a uniform methodology. This is the reason it is the foundation for all three papers that utilize the AMNE database (Borga et al. 2022; Zhang et al. 2020; Zhu, Guo, and Zhang 2022).

Yet, reliance on a single MRIO database also poses certain challenges. Reliance on the AMNE database focuses geographical coverage on Organisation for Economic Co-operation and Development (OECD) countries and time coverage no earlier than 2015 (due to data availability in the AMNE database). Additionally, calculating CO_2 emissions from fuel combustion using the International Energy Agency (IEA) estimates

BOX 2.3 Methodology for Estimating Carbon Emissions Using Top-Down Approaches

The multiregional input-output model (MRIO) extends a standard input-output matrix to a larger system with an independent row and column for each industry in each country. For instance, assuming that the world is composed of m countries and that each country has n sectors, the extended input-output matrix becomes

$$\begin{pmatrix} X_1 \\ X_2 \\ \vdots \\ X_m \end{pmatrix} = \begin{pmatrix} A_{11} & A_{12} & \cdots & A_{1m} \\ A_{21} & A_{22} & \cdots & A_{2m} \\ \vdots & \vdots & \ddots & \vdots \\ A_{m1} & A_{m2} & \cdots & A_{mm} \end{pmatrix} = \begin{pmatrix} X_1 \\ X_2 \\ \vdots \\ X_m \end{pmatrix} + \begin{pmatrix} Y_{11} \\ Y_{21} \\ \vdots \\ Y_{m1} \end{pmatrix}$$

$$X = AX + Y. \tag{1}$$

where X_i is the output of country i, A_{ii} is the intermediate requirements on domestic production in country i, A_{ij} is the interindustry requirements from country i to j, y_{ii} is the final demand for goods produced and consumed in region i, and y_{ij} is the final demand from region i to region j. By using the linearity assumptions from the model, equation (1) can be expressed as:

$$X = (I - A)^{-1}\,Y. \tag{2}$$

Since multinational enterprises (MNEs) can be part of different supply chain stages and the production technologies may be different between domestic and foreign-owned firms, a method is needed to trace the country's participation in global supply chains. For this, the literature offers two approaches: the *decomposition method* of the traditional Leontief model (Koopman et al. 2014) and the *hypothetical extraction method* that compares actual gross domestic product (GDP) in a country with a hypothetical GDP in case there are no production activities related to exporting (Los, Timmer, and de Vries 2016). Since both the decomposition method and the hypothetical extraction method reach the same results, the calculation of carbon emissions by MNEs is presented based on the decomposition method for sake of space.

(*Box continues on the following page.*)

BOX 2.3 Methodology to Estimating Carbon Emissions Using Top-Down Approaches (continued)

Following Zhang et al. (2020), assume that the production of each sector comprises the production of domestic-owned firms (D) and the production of foreign-owned firms (F). Thus, the final demand matrix Y and the intermediate input matrix A become:

$$Y=\begin{pmatrix} Y_{11}^{D} & Y_{12}^{D} & \cdots & Y_{1m}^{D} \\ Y_{21}^{F} & Y_{22}^{F} & \cdots & Y_{2m}^{F} \\ \vdots & \vdots & \ddots & \vdots \\ Y_{m1}^{D} & Y_{m2}^{D} & \cdots & Y_{mm}^{D} \\ Y_{m1}^{F} & Y_{m2}^{F} & \cdots & Y_{mm}^{F} \end{pmatrix}$$

$$A=\begin{pmatrix} Y_{11}^{DD} & Y_{12}^{DF} & \cdots & Y_{1m}^{DD} & Y_{1m}^{DF} \\ Y_{21}^{FD} & Y_{22}^{FF} & \cdots & Y_{2m}^{FD} & Y_{2m}^{FF} \\ \vdots & \vdots & \ddots & \vdots & \vdots \\ Y_{m1}^{DD} & Y_{m2}^{DF} & \cdots & Y_{mm}^{DD} & Y_{mm}^{DF} \\ Y_{m1}^{FD} & Y_{m2}^{FF} & \cdots & Y_{mm}^{FD} & Y_{mm}^{FF} \end{pmatrix}$$

where, for instance, A_{1m}^{DF} represents the direct requirements for the products of domestic firms in country 1 per unit of output of foreign-owned firms in country m.

To calculate the carbon emissions induced by the final demand, premultiply the right-hand side of equation (2) by the diagonal matrix E, which represents the carbon intensity matrix as follows:

$$C = E(I-A)^{-1}\,Y, \tag{3}$$

where the production-based emissions of each country are the sum of the matrix C by rows, and the consumption-based emissions of each country are the sum of the matrix C by columns. Additionally, to include the final and intermediate demand related to foreign-owned firms in a given country i, we can define the final demand matrix of products from MNEs as the intermediate demand ratio matrix of products from foreign-owned firms as A_i^{F*}. Likewise, we can define the final demand and the intermediate demand ratio matrix unrelated to MNEs in country i by Y_i^F and A_i^F, respectively.

On the basis that $A = A_i^F + A_i^{F*}$ and $Y = Y_i^F + Y_i^{F*}$, equation (3) can be expressed as follows:

$$C = E(I-A_i^F-A_i^{F*})^{-1}Y_i^F + E(I-A)^{-1}Y_{i.}^{F*} \tag{4}$$

From (4) and observing that $I-A=1-A_i^F-A_i^{F*}I=(I-A_i^F)^{-1}(I-A_{i.}^{F*})$, and $I=(I-A_i^F-A_i^{F*})^{-1}(I-A_i^F-A_{i.}^{F*})$, carbon footprints can be decomposed into three main components: emissions that are not related to the production activities of MNEs in country i (component 5.1), emissions embodied in the output of MNEs in country i that are used as intermediate inputs (component 5.2), and emissions embodied in the output of MNEs in country i that are used to satisfy final demand (component 5.3), as follows:

(Box continues on the following page.)

BOX 2.3 Methodology to Estimating Carbon Emissions Using Top-Down Approaches (continued)

$$\begin{aligned} C &= E(I-A_i^F)^{-1}Y_i^F + E(I-A_i^F)^{-1}A_i^{F^*}(I-A)^{-1}Y_i^F + E(I-A)^{-1}Y_i^{F^*}, \\ C &= (5.1) \qquad + (5.2) \qquad + (5.3) \end{aligned} \tag{5}$$

where components (5.2) and (5.3) correspond to the carbon emissions of the MNEs hosted by country *i*.

Furthermore, by defining the output of MNEs in country *i* that are used as intermediate inputs as $Z_i^{F^*} = A_i^{F^*}X$, the carbon emissions of the MNEs in country *i* becomes:

$$C_i^{host} = E(I-A+A_i^{F^*})^{-1}(Z_i^{F^*}+Y_i^{F^*}). \tag{6}$$

Finally, the change in the carbon footprints of MNEs in country *i* over a period can be expressed as

$$C_i^{host} = C_{i_t}^{host} - C_{i_0}^{host} = E_t B_{i_t}^{F^*} O_{i_t}^{F^*} - E_0 B_{i_0}^{F^*} O_{i_0}^{F^*}, \tag{7}$$

where $B_i^{F^*} = (I-A+A_i^{F^*})^{-1}$ represents the gross output of each sector required to produce per unit of output of the MNEs in country *i*, and $O_i^{F^*} = Z_i^{F^*} + Y_i^{F^*}$ is the output of the MNEs in country *i*. Zhang et al. (2020) use a polar decomposition of equation (7) to analyze the driving factors of carbon emissions of the MNEs hosted by a given country. Specifically, the decomposition gives rise to three drivers: the scale effect, carbon intensity (or technology) effect, and the production structure (or composition) effect. Algebraically, these are represented as follows:

$$\begin{aligned} \Delta C_i^{host} &= \tfrac{1}{2}\Delta O_{i_0}^{F^*}(E_0 B_{i_0}^{F^*} + E_t B_{i_t}^{F^*}) + \tfrac{1}{2}\Delta E(B_{i_t}^{F^*}O_{i_t}^{F^*} + B_{i0}^{F^*}O_{i_t}^{F^*}) + \tfrac{1}{2}\Delta B_{i_t}^{F^*}(E_0 O_{i_0}^{F^*} + E_t O_{i_t}^{F^*}) \\ \Delta C_i^{host} &= \text{(Scale Effect)} \qquad + \text{(Carbon Intensity Effect)} \quad + \text{(Production Structure Effect)}. \end{aligned} \tag{8}$$

Sources: World Bank based on Borga et al. 2022; Zhang et al. 2020; Zhu, Guo, and Zhang 2022.

does not exploit detailed country-specific information on emissions. Specifically, the IEA uses the simplest methodology to estimate CO_2 emissions, which offers comprehensive geographic coverage; however, it comes at the expense of disregarding more sophisticated tier 2 or tier 3 methods which are generally considered more accurate (Borga et al. 2022).[9]

In addition, the top-down approach also has a major data limitation due to the absence of detailed carbon emissions data for MNEs and non-MNEs. Due to data limitations, top-down estimates have to make very strong assumptions. Most notably they traditionally assume that MNEs and non-MNEs have similar carbon intensity within industries (which is clearly untrue, as shown in "Bottom-Up Approaches to Estimate the Effect of MNEs on Carbon Emissions" in this chapter).

The next few sections will present preliminary findings to consider the scale, technology, and composition effects of MNEs on climate change using top-down approaches.

Much of this analysis makes use of the International Monetary Fund's (IMF) Direct Investment-Related database from its Climate Change Indicators Dashboard, which covers carbon emissions embodied in the output of domestic and foreign owned enterprises, for 59 OECD countries, for the years 2005–2015. This is complemented with other recent studies that utilize the top-down approach.

Scale

López et al. (2019) find that US MNEs jointly make up a very large share of global emissions. To calculate the carbon footprint of US MNE foreign affiliates operating beyond the US borders, López and colleagues use the value added generated by the US-MNE abroad as an indicator of the generation of burden shifted income and emissions. They find that if US MNEs were a separate country, their direct emissions would rank them as the 12th top emitter of the world, responsible for 1.5 percent of the world's global emissions during 2009. However, this is a very conservative estimate, as it does not account for the large indirect effect MNEs may have on carbon emissions. López and colleagues further find that US-MNE carbon emissions vary depending on the country where the production takes place; MNEs pollute less heavily in European countries and more heavily in lower-income countries (in line with the pollution haven hypothesis; López et al. 2019).

Since MNEs can be part of different supply chain stages rather than being directly related to the final stages of production, Zhang et al. (2020), Borga et al. (2022), and Zhu, Guo, and Zhang (2022) study the role of MNEs in the entire supply chain. These authors use the AMNE database, which distinguishes among domestic firms, domestic MNEs (domestic firms with foreign affiliates), and foreign affiliates (firms with at least 50 percent foreign ownership). As the source of information related to carbon emissions, Zhang et al. (2020), Borga et al. (2022), and Zhu, Guo, and Zhang (2022) rely on sectoral CO_2 emissions data from the IEA. While each uses similar data as their foundations, their overall methodology and assumptions differ, leading to quite significant differences in results.

Zhang et al. (2020) suggest that the activities of MNEs have accounted for around 19–22 percent of global emissions and have been declining over time (figure 2.8). They find that total emissions rose between 2005 and 2008, when they reached their peak at 22 percent of global CO_2 emissions. While absolute emissions still grew somewhat over time, the relative share of MNE emissions declined every year and reached 18.7 percent of global emissions by 2016.

Borga et al. (2022) find that MNE output accounts for around 10 percent of global emissions, while its exports make up roughly 30 percent of export-related emissions. They estimate carbon emissions embodied in the output from domestic firms and MNEs operating in 59 (mostly OECD) countries from 2005 to 2015 (figure 2.9). This shows that emissions from MNEs have shown a small absolute increase during that

FIGURE 2.8 Emissions from MNEs' Supply Chains, 2005–15

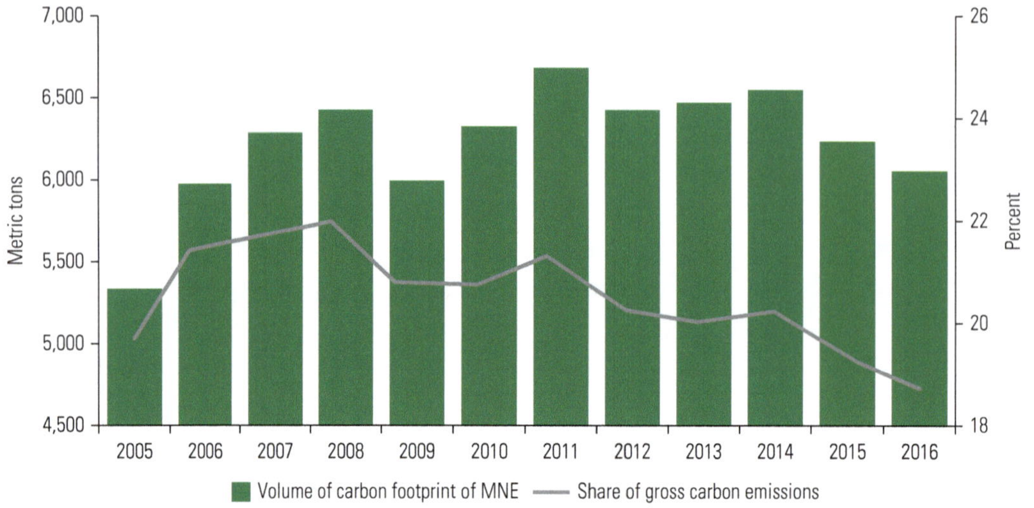

Source: Zhang et al. 2020.

Note: MNE = multinational enterprise.

FIGURE 2.9 Emissions from MNEs in Output and Exports, 2005–15

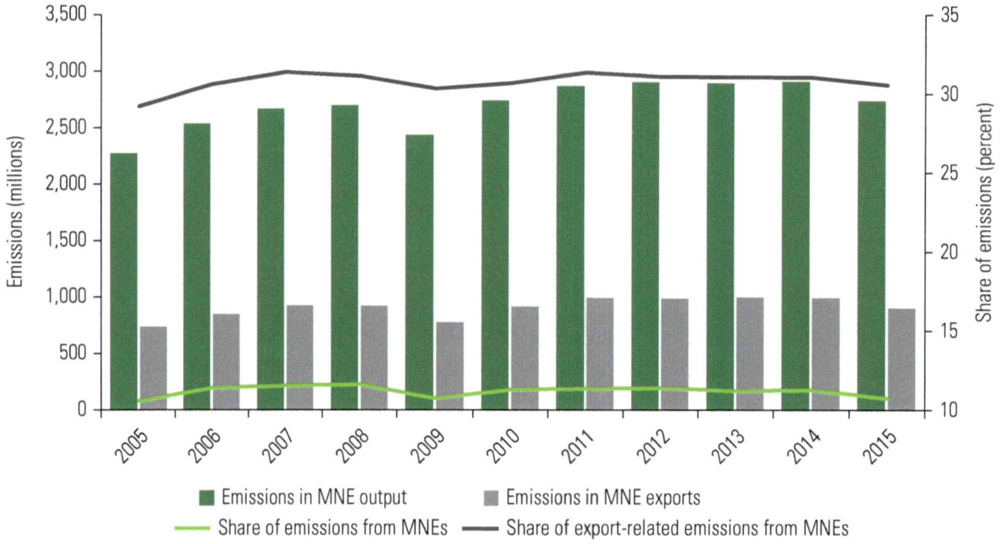

Source: World Bank calculations using data from Borga et al. 2022.

Note: MNE = multinational enterprise.

time, but their share of total emissions has stayed constant at around 10 percent. Emissions from MNEs' exports generally make up around one-third of MNE total emissions, and because MNEs are more likely to export than other firms, Borga et al. suggest that around one-third of total export-related emissions are due to the activities of MNEs.

Zhu, Guo, and Zhang (2022) find that the emissions generated by MNEs account for around 30 percent of emissions in high- and upper-middle-income countries and over 20 percent in lower-middle-income countries. Zhu, Guo, and Zhang (2022) conducted perhaps the most comprehensive top-down assessment of MNEs' impact on climate change. The authors decompose global emissions by domestic firms, conventional trade, and global value chains (GVCs). The latter category is usually driven by MNEs (Qiang, Liu, and Steenbergen 2021) and so provides a helpful way to identify emissions associated with MNEs' supply chains. As shown in table 2.2, they find that such GVCs account for around 30 percent of emissions in high- and upper-middle-income countries, and over 20 percent in lower-middle-income countries. The authors then further break GVC emissions down into three categories: GVC trade (MNE activities), GVC investment (FDI) and GVC trade and investment (MNE activities and FDI). Across all three income groups, most emissions are associated with GVC investment (FDI), accounting for around half of MNE emissions for high-income and upper-middle-income groups, and nearly 40 percent for lower-middle-income groups. Table 2.3 provides an additional breakdown specifically for emissions from GVC investment (FDI). Interestingly, this finds that for

TABLE 2.2 Emissions from Different Activities, by Economy Income

Year	Income level	Domestic firms (%)	Ricardian trade (%)	Global value chains			
				GVCs total (%)	GVC trade (MNEs) (%)	GVC investment (FDI) (%)	GVC trade and investment (MNEs and FDI) (%)
2005	High income	65.4	5.2	29.4	5.2	16.7	7.5
	Upper-middle income	61.7	7.1	31.3	9.4	12.8	9.1
	Lower-middle income	70.7	7.2	22.1	7.3	8.4	6.4
2016	High income	62.6	5.5	31.9	5.9	18.1	7.9
	Upper-middle income	66.4	5.9	27.7	6.7	13.6	7.4
	Lower-middle income	73.5	7.1	19.4	6.6	8.0	4.8

Source: World Bank–adjusted data based on Zhu, Guo, and Zhang 2022.

Note: FDI = foreign direct investment; GVCs = global value chains; MNEs = multinational enterprises.

TABLE 2.3 FDI-Related Emissions, by Economy Income Level

Year	Income Level	Total emissions from GVC investment (FDI) (%)	GVC investment emissions by type		
			MNEs' domestic production chains (%)	Joint production (MNEs and foreign firms) (%)	Joint production (MNEs and domestic firms) (%)
2005	High income	16.7	5.0	5.3	6.4
	Upper-middle income	12.8	2.5	3.3	7.0
	Lower-middle income	8.4	2.0	2.1	4.4
2016	High income	18.1	6.4	5.5	6.2
	Upper-middle income	13.6	2.1	3.0	8.4
	Lower-middle income	8.0	1.7	1.8	4.5

Source: World Bank–adjusted data based on Zhu, Guo, and Zhang 2022.
Note: FDI = foreign direct investment; GVC = global value chain; MNEs = multinational enterprises.

high-income countries, emissions are broadly split for MNEs' domestic production chains, joint production with foreign firms, and joint production with domestic firms. Yet, for other income categories, this is driven by joint production between MNEs and domestic firms. For upper-middle-income countries it accounts for 55–62 percent of MNEs' investment-related emissions, while for lower-middle-income countries this makes up 52–54 percent. This thus again stresses the important role played by MNEs in shaping the activities of domestic firms.

Technology

Data from Borga et al. (2022) paint a mixed picture about the carbon intensity of MNEs vis-à-vis domestic firms (figure 2.10). Using data from 59 countries from 2005 to 2015 in 34 industries based on International Standard Industrial Classification of All Economic Activities (ISIC) revision 4, Borga et al. (2022) find that production in MNEs pollutes less than domestic firms in several sectors, including electricity and gas, mining and quarrying, and coke and petroleum products. Yet, sectors such as transport and storage, and manufacturing subsectors such as textile and apparel, fabricated metal products, computer and electronics products, machinery and equipment, motor vehicles, and textiles and apparel do not follow this pattern, and MNEs appear more polluting than domestic firms. It is important to note, however, that due to data limitations, the direct emission intensities of MNEs were assumed to be the same as domestic firms in the same industry (a very strong assumption, as discussed in "Bottom-Up Approaches to Estimate the Effect of MNEs on Carbon Emissions" in this chapter). The variation in emissions across firm types is mainly due to differences in their industry distribution and sourcing patterns especially between domestic and imported inputs. Better data on the emissions of MNEs (for example, from CDP data), would likely result in showing larger differences between estimates of their carbon intensity (Borga et al. 2022).

FIGURE 2.10 Carbon Intensity of Output, 2005–15, Selected Sectors

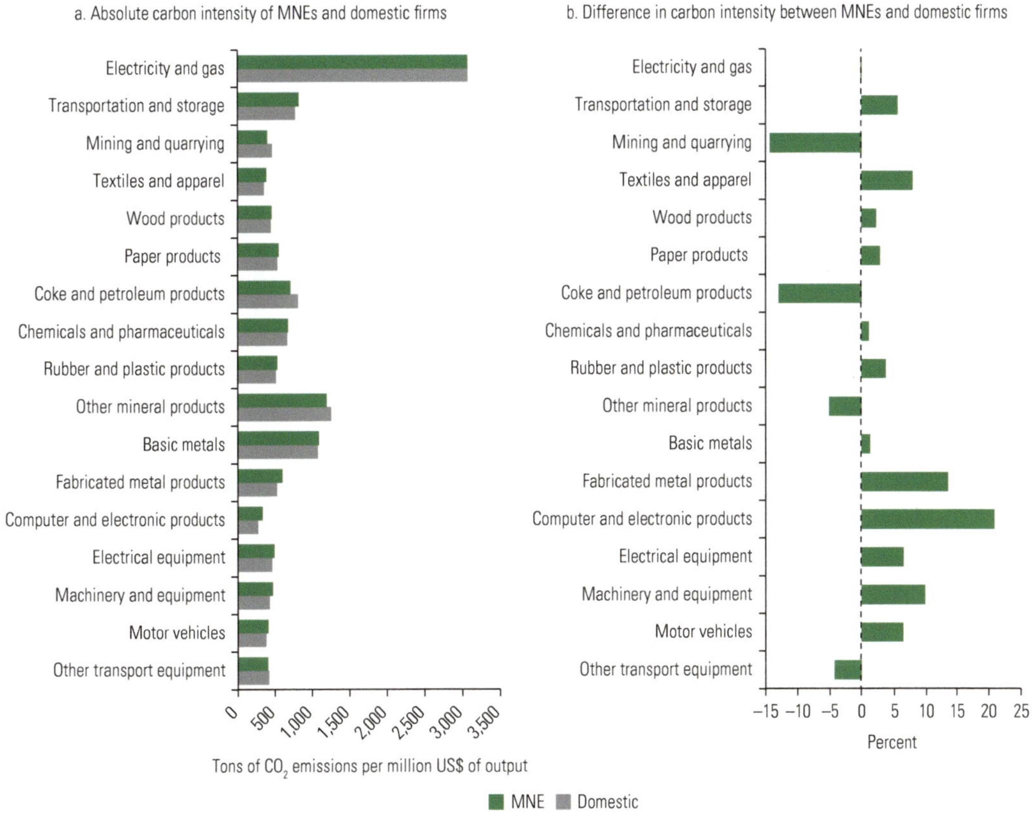

Sources: World Bank calculations based on IMF data; Borga et al. 2022.
Note: CO_2 = carbon dioxide; IMF = International Monetary Fund; MNE = multinational enterprise.

Composition

Zhang et al. (2020) provide a powerful decomposition of the effect of MNEs across the scale, technology, and composition channels (figure 2.11). They study the driving factors of the carbon footprints of MNEs hosted by each country over time by decomposing the overall emissions into the three effects: (a) the scale effect (FDI-led increase of economic activity); (b) the carbon intensity effect (FDI-led use and diffusion of low-carbon technology); and (c) the composition effect (FDI-led change of industrial structure composition).[10] These results powerfully illustrate the fact that MNEs provide both challenges and opportunities for climate change. It first shows that the role of MNEs has changed over time. They contributed to the growth of emissions from 2005 until 2008 (+20.4 percent) and 2008 until 2011 (+4 percent). The major contributing factor to this increase was the growth in the outputs of MNEs (scale effect), which would cause the carbon footprints of MNEs to increase by 27.4 percent in the

FIGURE 2.11 Emissions Embodied in the Supply Chains of MNEs: Scale, Technology, and Composition Effects

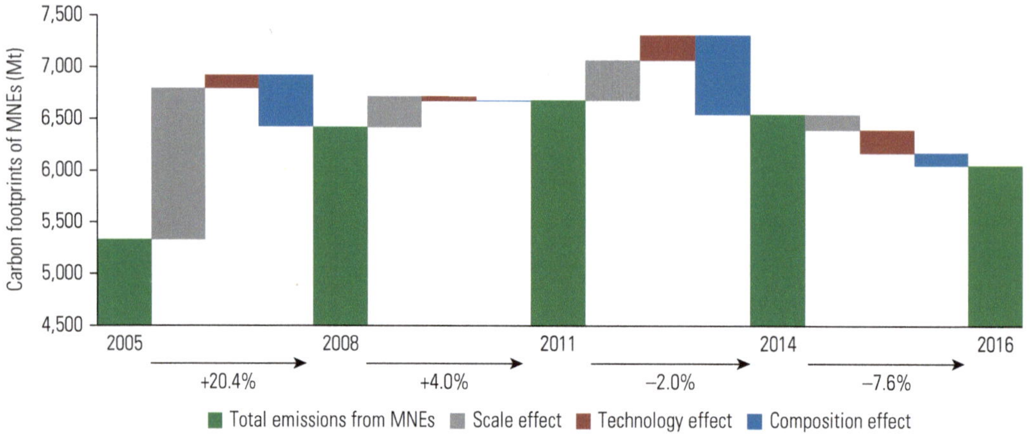

Source: World Bank based on Zhang et al. 2020.
Note: MNEs = multinational enterprises; Mt = metric tons.

absence of other factors. The decrease in carbon intensity offset the carbon footprints of MNEs by −9.3 percent (intensity effect), and the change in production technology played a relatively modest role (+2.4 percent, technology effect). Yet, they have since become a net reducer of carbon emissions. From 2011 to 2014, MNEs showed a 2 percent decline in emissions, and from 2014 to 2016 their footprint declined by 7.6 percent. Over the period 2011–2014, both the scale effect (+5.8 percent) and the technology effect (+3.7 percent) played important roles in driving the carbon footprints of MNEs. This is partly because the volume of global FDI shrank, while MNEs began to adopt measures to clean up their supply chains. Over the subperiod 2014–2016, all three effects contributed to the declining carbon footprints of MNEs. The changes in output, production technology, and carbon intensity of MNEs would contribute to a decline in their carbon footprints of −2.3 percent, −3.4 percent and −1.9 percent, respectively, with all other factors held constant (Zhang et al. 2020). This, in turn, shows the important and countervailing effects of the three channels: scale, technology, and composition.

In conclusion, this chapter has illustrated the strong role that MNEs play in climate change. The climate change literature has often presented the activities of MNEs either as a risk to increase emissions to developing countries by shifting their polluting activities to locations with limited environmental regulation (pollution haven), or as an opportunity to reduce emissions in developing countries by attracting cleaner technology (pollution halo). However, this binary view is too simplistic. New analysis using micro- and macro-data on GHG emissions allows us to map the effect of MNEs more closely and showcases that they can bring with them both challenges and opportunities

BOX 2.4 **Future Research Agenda—Strengthen Estimates of MNEs' Effect on Emissions by Harmonizing Top-Down and Bottom-Up Approaches**

This chapter provides an initial assessment of the effect of MNEs on climate change. Yet, to better understand the role of MNEs in climate change, there could be significant benefits in harmonizing top-down and bottom-up approaches. The top-down approaches have the benefit of avoiding double-counting emissions within supply chains. Yet, they currently cannot differentiate the carbon intensity of MNEs and non-MNEs at the country-industry level. Bottom-up approaches that use firm-level data can enable estimation models to reflect the differences in carbon-intensity between different groups of firms, such as between MNEs and non-MNEs, and across sectors. This type of approach would therefore utilize the best of both worlds, avoiding double-counting emissions across supply chains but incorporating heterogenous firm-level dynamics for the biggest firms across each country and industry. Jointly, this would likely provide the most accurate and realistic estimates of the role of MNEs on climate change.

for climate change mitigation. We found that a small number of MNEs are major drivers of global GHG emissions. However, their technologies have also helped reduce carbon emissions for themselves and their supply chains. Similarly, global investment is increasingly pouring into green sectors, thereby further facilitating the green transition of industry. Jointly, we can think about this in terms of scale, technology, and composition effects of MNEs on GHG emissions. Finally, to better understand the impact of MNEs on climate change, we argue that there may be a benefit to harmonizing top-down and bottom-up approaches (see box 2.4). This is an important research agenda going forward.

Notes

1. For more details about the Climate Action 100+, see https://www.climateaction100.org/. Climate Action 100+ focused on 166 companies, but sufficient information for this analysis was available for only 157. Using a small number of MNEs also reduces problems associated with aggregating scope 3 emissions for firms within the same value chain. Yet, issues may still remain (for example, potential double counting of emissions from energy use).
2. The Organisation for Economic Co-operation and Development's (OECD) Annual Greenhouse Gas (GHG) Air Emissions Accounts separates two emissions categories: industrial and household. In 2021, industrial emissions accounted for 89 percent of total anthropogenic emissions (45.6 billion metric tons carbon-dioxide equivalent, CO_2e).
3. A reason for this is that it attributes scope 3 emissions to the location of the MNE overseeing the production of the value chain rather than the more commonly reported country-level consumption of goods and services.
4. Regression analysis suggests that being an MNE is associated with a statistically significant 54 percent lower CO_2e use per metric ton of crude steel production for basic oxygen furnaces, but no significant effects for the other technologies (likely due to the low number of observations). See table 2A.2 in annex 2A for details.

5. Examples of such low CO_2 cement include injecting CO_2, fly ash, or steel slag into cement during mixing. By permanently embedding it in the concrete it strengthens it—thereby reducing the emissions in the production process and reducing the amount of cement needed (Zero Energy Project 2020).
6. Regression analysis suggests that being an MNE is associated with a statistically significant lower CO_2e use per metric ton of cement production for clinkers (−3.6%), cementitious products (−9.2%) and low-CO_2 materials (−210%). See table 2A.3 in annex 2A for details.
7. It is important to note, also, that these estimates are likely significantly underestimating the effect of MNEs on carbon intensity, as the sample only includes firms who chose to voluntarily include themselves in CDP's emissions dataset, and are generally larger and more committed to climate change mitigation. According to Bolton and Kacperczyk (2022), such firms already have considerably lower carbon intensity than the universe of firms.
8. The AMNE database links the OECD Inter-Country Input-Output (ICIO) and the Trade in Value Added databases.
9. The 2006 IPCC Guidelines for National Greenhouse Gas Inventories (Eggleston et al. 2006) provide methodologies for estimating national inventories of anthropogenic emissions by sources and removals by sinks of greenhouse gases. The 2006 IPCC Guidelines provide advice on estimations methods at three levels of detail. Tier 1 is an approach that uses spatially rough default data based on globally available data. Tier 2 is a more accurate approach that substitutes the general defaults for country- or region-specific values and more disaggregated activity data. And tier 3 is a more sophisticated method that involves detailed modeling and inventory measurement systems driven by data at a greater resolution. Tiers 2 and 3 are more accurate but demand more information and better data quality (Eggleston et al. 2006).
10. See box 2.3, "Methodology to Estimating Carbon Emissions Using Top-Down Approaches," for further details.

References

Adeel-Farooq, R. M., M. F. Riaz, and T. Ali. 2021. "Improving the Environment Begins at Home: Revisiting the Links Between FDI and Environment." *Energy* 215: 119150.

Benzerrouk Z., M. Abid, and H. Sekrafi. 2021. "Pollution Haven or Halo Effect? A Comparative Analysis of Developing and Developed Countries." *Energy Reports* 7: 4862–71.

Bolton, Patrick, and Marcin T. Kacperczyk. 2022. "Firm Commitments." Research Paper, Columbia Business School, New York.

Borga, M., A. Pegoue, G. Henri, A. Sanchez, D. Entaltsev, and K. Egesa. 2022. "Measuring Carbon Emissions of Foreign Direct Investment in Host Countries." IMF Working Paper WP/22/86, International Monetary Fund, Washington, DC.

CDP (formerly the Carbon Disclosure Project). 2020. "CDP Full GHG Emissions Dataset—Technical Annex." CDP, London.

CDP. 2022a. CDP Full GHG Emissions Dataset 2022: Summary. CDP, London. https://www.cdp.net/en/investor/ghg-emissions-dataset.

CDP. 2022b. CDP Corporate Response Data.

Chava, S. 2014. "Environmental Externalities and Cost of Capital." *Management Science* 60 (9): 2223–47.

Duan, Y., and X. Jiang. 2021. "Pollution Haven or Pollution Halo? A Re-Evaluation on the Role of Multinational Enterprises in Global CO_2 Emissions." *Energy Economics* 97: 105181.

The Economist. 2022. "New Technology Can Help Monitor, Manage and Minimise Methane Leaks." *Economist Technology Quarterly*, June 23, 2022 (updated June 24, 2022).

Eggleston H. S., L. Buendia, K. Miwa, T. Ngara, and K. Tanabe, eds. 2006. *2006 IPCC Guidelines for National Greenhouse Gas Inventories.* Hayama, Japan: Institute for Global Environmental Strategies (IGES).

European Commission. (2020). Regulation (European Union [EU]) 2020/852 of the European Parliament and of the Council of 18 June 2020 on the establishment of a framework to facilitate sustainable investment, and amending Regulation (EU) 2019/2088 (text with EEA relevance).

Hanif, I., S. M. F. Raza, P. Gago-de-Santos, and Q. Abbas. 2019. "Fossil Fuels, Foreign Direct Investment, and Economic Growth Have Triggered CO_2 Emissions in Emerging Asian Economies: Some Empirical Evidence." *Energy* 171: 493–501.

Heede, R. 2014. "Tracing Anthropogenic Carbon Dioxide and Methane Emissions to Fossil Fuel and Cement Producers, 1854–2010." *Climatic Change* 122 (1): 229–41.

IRENA (International Renewable Energy Agency). 2020. "How Falling Costs Make Renewables a Cost-effective Investment." https://www.irena.org/newsroom/articles/2020/Jun/How-Falling-Costs-Make-Renewables-a-Cost-effective-Investment.

Koçak, E., and A Şarkgüneşi. 2018. "The Impact of Foreign Direct Investment on CO_2 Emissions in Turkey: New Evidence from Cointegration and Bootstrap Causality Analysis." *Environmental Science and Pollution Research* 25(1): 790–804.

Koopman, Robert, Zhi Wang, and Shang-Jin Wei. 2014. "Tracing Value-added and Double Counting in Gross Exports." *American Economic Review* 104 (2): 459–94.

López, L. A., M. Á. Cadarso, J. Zafrilla, and G. Arce. 2019. "The Carbon Footprint of the US Multinationals' Foreign Affiliates." *Nature Communications* 10 (1): 1–11.

Los, B., M. P. Timmer, and G. J. de Vries. 2016. "Tracing Value-Added and Double Counting in Gross Exports: Comment." *American Economic Review* 106 (7): 1958–66.

Nasir, Muhammad Ali, Toan Huynh, and Tram Huong. 2019. "Role of Financial Development, Economic Growth & Foreign Direct Investment in Driving Climate Change: A Case of Emerging ASEAN." *Journal of Environmental Management* 242: 131–41.

OECD (Organisation for Economic Co-operation and Development). 2022. *FDI Qualities Policy Toolkit.* Paris: OECD Publishing. https://doi.org/10.1787/7ba74100-en.

Qiang, Christine Zhenwei, Yan Liu, and Victor Steenbergen. 2021. *An Investment Perspective on Global Value Chains.* Washington, DC: World Bank. https://openknowledge.worldbank.org/handle/10986/35526.

Sapkota, P., and U. Bastola. 2017. "Foreign Direct Investment, Income, and Environmental Pollution in Developing Countries: Panel Data Analysis of Latin America." *Energy Economics* 64: 206–12.

Shahbaz, M., I. Haouas, and T. H. Van Hoang. 2019. "Economic Growth and Environmental Degradation in Vietnam: Is the Environmental Kuznets Curve a Complete Picture?" *Emerging Markets Review* 38: 197–218.

Solarin, S. A., U. Al-Mulali, I. Musah, and I. Ozturk. 2017. "Investigating the Pollution Haven Hypothesis in Ghana: An Empirical Investigation." *Energy* 124: 706–19.

Tang, C. F., and B. W. Tan. 2015. "The Impact of Energy Consumption, Income and Foreign Direct Investment on Carbon Dioxide Emissions in Vietnam." *Energy* 79: 447–54.

Waqih, M. A. U., N. A. Bhutto, N. H. Ghumro, S. Kumar, and M. A. Salam. 2019. "Rising Environmental Degradation and Impact of Foreign Direct Investment: Empirical Evidence from SAARC Region." *Journal of Environmental Management* 243: 472–80.

World Resources Institute (WRI) and the World Business Council for Sustainable Development (WBCSD). 2004. *The Greenhouse Gas Protocol. A Corporate Accounting and Reporting Standard.* Washington, DC: WRI and Conches-Geneva, Switzerland: WBCSD.

Zero Energy Project. 2020. "Low Carbon Concrete—Starting from the Ground Up." *Zero Energy Project Blog*, November 9, 2020. https://zeroenergyproject.org/2020/11/09/low-carbon-concrete-starting-from-the-ground-up/.

Zhang, Z. D. Guan, R. Wang, J. Meng, H. Zheng, K. Zhu, and H. Du. 2020. "Embodied Carbon Emissions in the Supply Chains of Multinational Enterprises." *Nature Climate Change* 10 (12): 1096–101.

Zhu, H., L. Duan, Y. Guo, and K. Yu. 2016. "The Effects of FDI, Economic Growth and Energy Consumption on Carbon Emissions in ASEAN-5: Evidence from Panel Quantile Regression." *Economic Modelling* 58: 237–48.

Zhu, K., X. Guo, and Z. Zhang. 2022. "Reevaluation of the Carbon Emissions Embodied in Global Value Chains Based on an Inter-country Input-Output Model with Multinational Enterprises." *Applied Energy* 307: 118220.

Annex 2A. Additional Methodological Details and Regression Tables

Methodology for Apportioning Emissions across MNE Affiliates

Step 1: Download raw list of each MNE's affiliates. Identify the global structure of 157 MNEs by using Orbis's database of subsidiaries. The company was manually identified in Orbis (matched on name and headquarters' location), and then their list of subsidiaries was downloaded (including only those subsidiaries with a majority ownership for the MNE). This provides a total list of 57,605 affiliates.

Step 2: Drop affiliates without economic data. We kept only those subsidiaries which reported on at least one of the following three indicators: operational revenue, total assets, and number of employees. This leaves a total of 19,600 affiliates.

Step 3: Impute missing values for affiliates missing one or two of the three economic figures. The reported data of economic activities of affiliates are heavily unbalanced: 28 percent of firms miss revenue figures, 29 percent miss asset figures, and 36 percent miss employment figures. To deal with this partial reporting for subsidiaries, we use simple multiple imputation methods to fill missing observations. We run separate regressions for each MNE and estimate the average relationship for their affiliates between the three variables (revenue, assets, and employment) and use these to impute missing observations.

Step 4: Apportion each MNE's scope 1, 2, and 3 global emissions to their affiliates based on the specific set of activities. Finally, we rely on each MNE affiliate's relative share in the company's total assets, revenue, and employment to apportion their global emissions. To do so, we provide a crude approximation based on the specific type of activities related to their scope 1, 2, and 3 emissions and pair these to one of the three economic indicators. For example, scope 3 emissions associated with capital goods are apportioned proportionate to each affiliate's relative share of assets, while scope 3 emissions associated with employee commuting is apportioned proportionate to the affiliate's relative share of employment. The full breakdown of each emission activity is provided in table 2A.1.

TABLE 2A.1 Approach for Apportioning Emissions across MNE Affiliates

Type of activity	Scope	Type of activity	Apportioning across MNE affiliates
Upstream activities	Scope 3	Purchased goods and services	Assets + employment
		Capital goods	Assets
		Fuel-and-energy-related activities (not included in scope 1 or 2)	Assets + employment
		Upstream transportation and distribution	Assets + employment
		Waste generated in operations	Assets + employment
		Business travel	Employment
		Employee commuting	Employment
		Upstream leased assets	Assets
		Other (upstream)	Assets + employment
	Scope 2	Purchased electricity, steam, and heating and cooling for own use	Assets + employment
Reporting company	Scope 1	Company facilities and vehicles	Assets + employment
Downstream activities	Scope 3	Downstream transportation and distribution	Revenue
		Processing of sold products	Revenue
		Use of sold products	Revenue
		End of life treatment of sold products	Revenue
		Downstream leased assets	Assets
		Franchises	Revenue
		Investments	Assets
		Other (downstream)	Revenue

Sources: World Bank based on CDP and Orbis data.

Note: CDP = formerly the Carbon Disclosure Project; MNE = multinational enterprise.

Additional Regression Tables on Technology Intensity for Steel and Cement and MNEs

TABLE 2A.2 Regression Table: Metric Tons CO_2e per Metric Ton of Crude Steel Production

Variables	(1)	(2)	(3)
	Blast furnace: basic oxygen furnace	Direct reduced iron-electric arc furnace	Scrap-electric arc furnace
MNEs	−0.542**	−0.540	−0.118
	(0.211)	(0.620)	(0.137)
Constant	2.216***	1.125**	0.660***
	(0.0991)	(0.205)	(0.0932)
Observations	18	4	23
R-squared	0.232	0.275	0.034

Sources: World Bank based on CDP and Orbis data.

Note: CDP = formerly the Carbon Disclosure Project; CO_2e = carbon dioxide equivalent; MNEs = multinational enterprises. Robust standard errors in parentheses.

*** $p < 0.01$, ** $p < 0.05$, * $p < 0.1$.

TABLE 2A.3 Regression Table: Metric Tons CO_2e per Metric Ton of Cement Production

Variables	(1)	(2)	(3)	(4)
	Clinkers	Cement equivalent	Cementitious products	Low-CO_2 materials
MNEs	−0.0357*	−0.0561	−0.0915*	−2.104*
	(0.0197)	(0.0434)	(0.0468)	(0.993)
Constant	0.876***	0.666***	0.685***	2.510***
	(0.0184)	(0.0291)	(0.0290)	(0.759)
Observations	23	22	23	12
R-squared	0.157	0.070	0.142	0.310

Sources: World Bank based on CDP and Orbis data.

Note: CDP = formerly the Carbon Disclosure Project; CO_2 = carbon dioxide; MNEs = multinational enterprises. Robust standard errors in parentheses.

*** $p < 0.01$, ** $p < 0.05$, * $p < 0.1$

3. Multinational Enterprises and Green Technology Transfers

The Potential of Green Technology Transfers

The previous chapter illustrated the importance of the technology channel as a way for multinational enterprises (MNEs) to reduce industrial carbon emissions. Estimates of carbon intensities of final demand for products produced by MNEs vis-à-vis domestic firms show that MNEs have lower carbon intensities than that of domestic firms in almost all industries and countries. Thus, it may be expected that an eventual diffusion of environment-friendly technologies from MNEs to domestic firms will benefit local communities. This section looks into green technology transfers more broadly and considers how MNEs currently shape such transfers.

The stock of technological equipment, know-how, and capabilities of technology owners is concentrated in a few developed economies. Developed countries account for more than 70 percent of global research and development (R&D) expenditure and have more stringent environmental regulations—factors that explain higher innovation-led development as well as deployment of green technologies. Patent data analysis shows that only a handful of countries, such as Germany, Japan, and the United States account for two-thirds of climate-friendly innovations (Dechezleprêtre et al. 2011). As a result, those countries possess the vast majority of proprietary technologies, often with intellectual property protections that limit avenues for application in developing countries.

The transfer of green technologies to developing countries, at the desired scale for global climate action, is neither rapid nor automatic. Green technologies do diffuse from developed to developing economies, albeit slowly. This is likely because of the challenges in simultaneously preserving the interests of technology owners (concentrated in developed countries) and of their recipient users. Although slow, the diffusion of technology across countries does occur (Popp 2011) and is mainly driven by the declining costs of technology over time. As the cost of emissions reduction falls, it makes environmental regulations in developing countries more feasible to enforce. Similar to developed countries, the combination of access to technology (at lower cost) and environmental regulations incentivizes the adoption of green technologies in developing countries (Lovely and Popp 2011).

The extent to which developing countries can access and deploy green technologies depends on their integration into global value chains and the potential to adapt technologies for local use.[1] The patterns of green technology transfer are different in emerging and low-income countries (Glachant et al. 2013). Emerging economies are more integrated into global production networks and benefit from inward technology transfers enshrined in imported goods and through investments by MNEs. Emerging economies, some evidence suggests, also contribute to the development of green technologies. Brazil, China, the Republic of Korea, and the Russian Federation together accounted for about 18 percent of climate-friendly innovations and about 7 percent of high-value patents (that is, patent applications filed in multiple countries) globally between 2000 and 2005 (Dechezleprêtre et al. 2011). Low-income countries, however, are much more constrained: they import fewer green technologies, in large part because they have not yet developed the capabilities to deploy them productively (Mealy and Teytelboym 2020). According to Pigato et al. (2020) we can distinguish between three main sources of green technology transfers: foreign direct investment (FDI), imports, and licensing. We will discuss each in turn.

Technology Transfers from FDI

FDI provides an important avenue for firms in developing countries to access new technologies and approaches that have been researched and deployed successfully in advanced economies. Foreign parent firms from developed economies often transfer firm-specific technology and know-how to their affiliates in developing countries (Arnold and Javorcik 2009; Branstetter, Fisman, and Foley 2006; Saurav and Kuo 2020). Such transfers of specialized know-how can materialize because for the parent firm, the ownership stake and implied control over the affiliate lowers the risk of technology leakage (Djankov and Hoekman 2000).

Recent evidence suggests that foreign ownership can be an important driver of the shift toward more environmentally sustainable practices, in particular for small firms that operate in sectors that are less regulated. Balaguer, Cuadros, and García-Quevedo (2022), using data on Spanish manufacturing firms, find positive effects of foreign ownership on both investments and current expenditures in environmental protection. These effects are especially relevant for smaller firms, in which foreign investment helps finance the necessary upgrades to become more environmentally sustainable. MNE involvement also led to increased adoption of environmental measures for firms in industrial sectors with less stringent environmental regulations. Hence foreign capital in firms can overcome barriers related to financial resources, technology, and managerial skills and thereby increase actions related to environmental protection. Similarly, survey evidence from Saurav et al. (2021) suggests that during the COVID-19 (coronavirus) pandemic, foreign parent firms actively supported their affiliates in developing countries to adopt sustainability and decarbonization measures.

Technology Transfers from Imports

Importing capital goods provides a rapid conduit for technology transfer as trade can move physical products (which are embodied technologies) between locations relatively quickly. Trade enables developing countries to tap into the productivity-enhancing global stock of knowledge to access intermediate goods and capital equipment that they could not produce domestically otherwise (Pigato et al. 2020). However, trade does not necessarily facilitate cross-border transfer of knowledge. Since knowledge is located and leveraged in the exporting country, the flow of disembodied technology transfer through knowledge is limited (Glachant et al. 2013). Knowledge spillovers may still occur to the extent that firms in the importing countries can reverse-engineer imported technologies (Rivera-Batiz and Romer 1991).[2]

Despite a leveling off in recent years, global trade data suggest that trade of green technologies has increased manyfold in recent decades. Since 1990 this value has increased from US$43.6 billion to US$ 809.9 billion in 2017—a 20-fold increase (Pigato et al. 2020; figure 3.1, panel a). While income per capita is positively correlated with imports of green technology, lower-income countries have participated substantially in this trend. When holding the 1992 income group classification fixed, imports of green technology by lower-income countries has risen markedly and particularly so for those countries that have moved into higher income categories (Pigato et al. 2020; figure 3.1, panel b). In 1992, only 23 of 125 low-income and lower-middle-income countries were importing low-carbon technology products. By 2016, 53 of 84 (about two-thirds) of countries classified as low income or lower-middle income were importing that type of technology.

FIGURE 3.1 Change in Green Technology Trade Globally and in Developing Countries

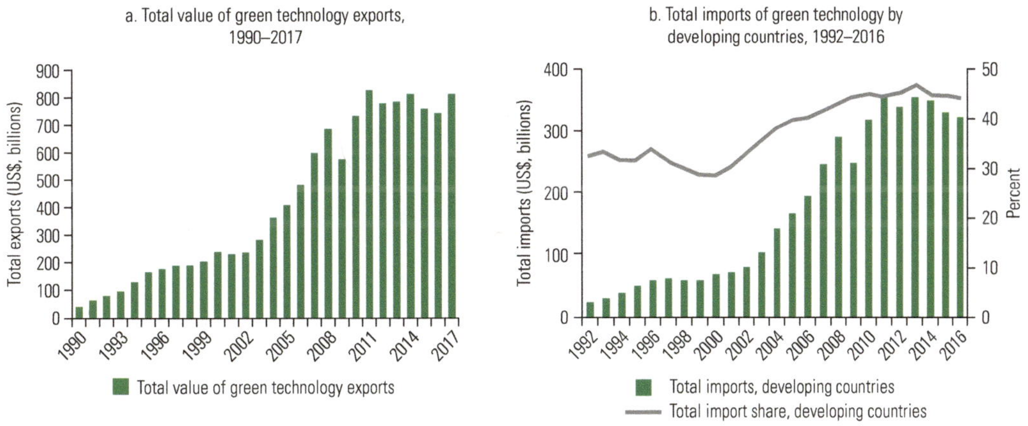

Source: Pigato et al. 2020.

Developing countries rely heavily on developed countries for green technologies, but emerging economies are increasingly becoming a source of technology transfers. Exports from developed countries to developing countries have grown substantially in the past two decades and account for one-quarter of global trade in green technologies. Meanwhile, trade between developing countries accounted for only about 11 percent of total global exports and only 9 percent of total green technology exports (Pigato et al. 2020). A few emerging economies—namely, Brazil, China, India, Korea, Mexico, and South Africa—play a large role in both absorbing green technologies and contributing to their production and diffusion to other developing countries. For instance, China and Korea have excelled in absorbing these technologies, which has spurred domestic innovation and thus enabled them to become two of the top five exporters of green technologies to developing countries (Pigato et al. 2020). Others, such as Brazil and Mexico, have integrated into some global value chains related to green technology (for example, automotive). These and a few other emerging economies first imported more green technologies than they exported, after which exports began to grow (figure 3.2 panels a and b), suggesting that trade has facilitated some level of knowledge spillover in these countries.

Technology Transfers from Licensing

A direct channel of technology transfer is when an MNE grants a patent license to a firm in another country, which can then use the licensed technology to upgrade its operations. Licensing enables MNEs to avoid trade barriers to certain technologies and

FIGURE 3.2 Total Green Technology Imports and Exports for Select Emerging Economies, 1992–2016

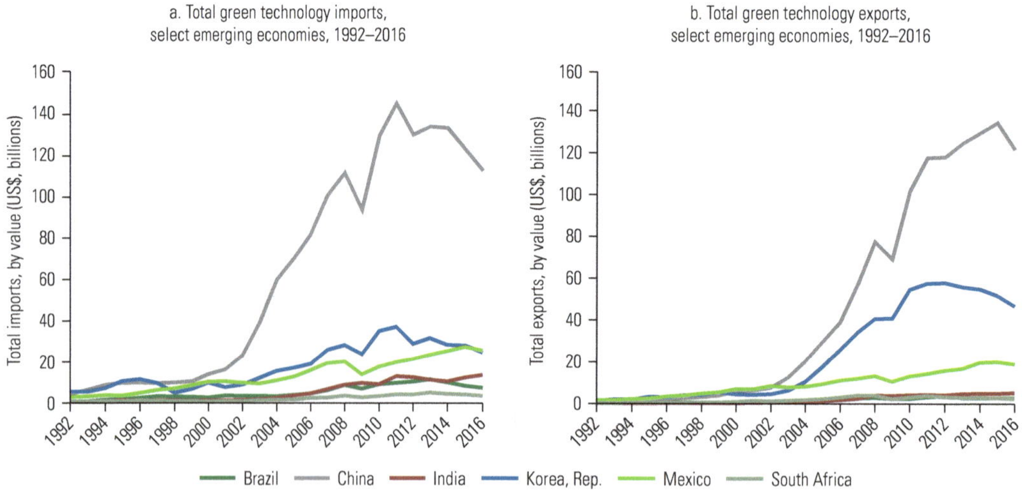

Source: Pigato et al. 2020.

enter less familiar countries (Popp 2011). Licensing facilitates knowledge transfer to the licensee firm, implying that the licensor may give up some control over the technology. Intellectual property rights play an important role here by securing technology leakage. Licensing relationships, secured by intellectual property protections, can be a conduit of technology transfers. Stronger intellectual property rights allow MNEs to protect their technology, thereby reducing risks and raising the willingness to license it. At the same time, stronger intellectual property rights may make knowledge transfer less likely (Popp 2011). This may likely be a reason MNEs tend to transfer newer technologies that are more susceptible to technology leakage through FDI relationships, whereas older less cutting-edge technologies are more frequently the subject of licensing arrangements (Mansfield and Romeo 1980; Saggi 1999).

Data on licensing trends are limited, but licensing fee payments from developing to developed countries grew fivefold between 1999 and 2006 (World Bank 2008). Various examples illustrate the role of licensing in green technology transfer to developing countries. Licensing agreements with European manufacturers to access wind turbine technology were a critical first step for both China and India in building up their own R&D efforts in the wind power industry (Lewis 2007; Ru et al. 2012). The solar power industries in these two countries have also benefited. A California-based solar thermal startup, eSolar, entered into exclusive master licensing agreements with India's ACME Group in 2009 and China's Penglai Electric Company in 2010 for their turnkey solar power plant solution (Lane 2010). (At the time, it was China's largest solar thermal project.) A final example is that, as of 2009, General Electric had licensed its coal gasification technology to 40 facilities in China (Lane 2010).

Links with MNEs Associated with Greener Business Practices

This section considers how different interactions between domestic firms and MNEs (via investment, partnership, and trade) affect domestic firms' green technology transfers. This analysis makes use of the World Bank Enterprise Survey's new Green Economy Module, which is available for 30 countries in Eastern Europe and Central Asia, and 6 countries in the Middle East and Northern Africa. The surveys were conducted between 2018 and 2020 and provide information on nine green firm characteristics about firms' strategic objectives and target setting, monitoring, and implementation measures. To consider the effect of MNE interactions, we conduct simple firm-level regressions based on foreign ownership, international supply links, and international licensing. Each regression controls for country, sector, and year fixed effects as well as several covariates such as firm age and size. Because the data are only available as a cross-section, the analysis does suffer from endogeneity problems, and so it is not possible to obtain causal estimates. As such, the results should be interpreted as suggestive only.

Descriptive statistics suggest that firms linked to MNEs through supply links, equity partnerships, or technological licensing arrangements are more likely to adopt green business practices, as compared to their peers without such links (figure 3.3). On average, we see that foreign-owned firms are most likely to adopt green practices, followed by firms linked to MNEs in other ways. Domestic firms without such links are the least likely to engage in green practices. These differences are particularly marked in the adoption of measures to control pollution, where nearly 70 percent of foreign-owned firms implement such measures as compared to about 10 percent in domestic firms with no links. Differences also persist in areas that generate direct cost savings for firms, such as energy-saving measures. So, links with MNEs have the potential to contribute to greening business practices in domestic businesses.

Equity partnerships with foreign firms (joint ventures) stimulate firms to incorporate climate change into their strategic objectives and their monitoring but not to undertake implementation measures to improve their environmental performance. Table 3.1 shows a significant and positive association between equity partnerships with foreign firms and some green performance indicators, including strategic objective and target setting, monitoring energy consumption, and having a manager who is responsible for environmental issues. However, such joint ventures are not associated with any significant impact on implementation measures.

Supply links have a sizeable impact on firms' adoption of strategic objectives for climate change and target setting, monitoring, and implementation measures. Table 3.2 presents

FIGURE 3.3 Firms' Adoption of Green Business Practices, by Type of MNE Link, 2020

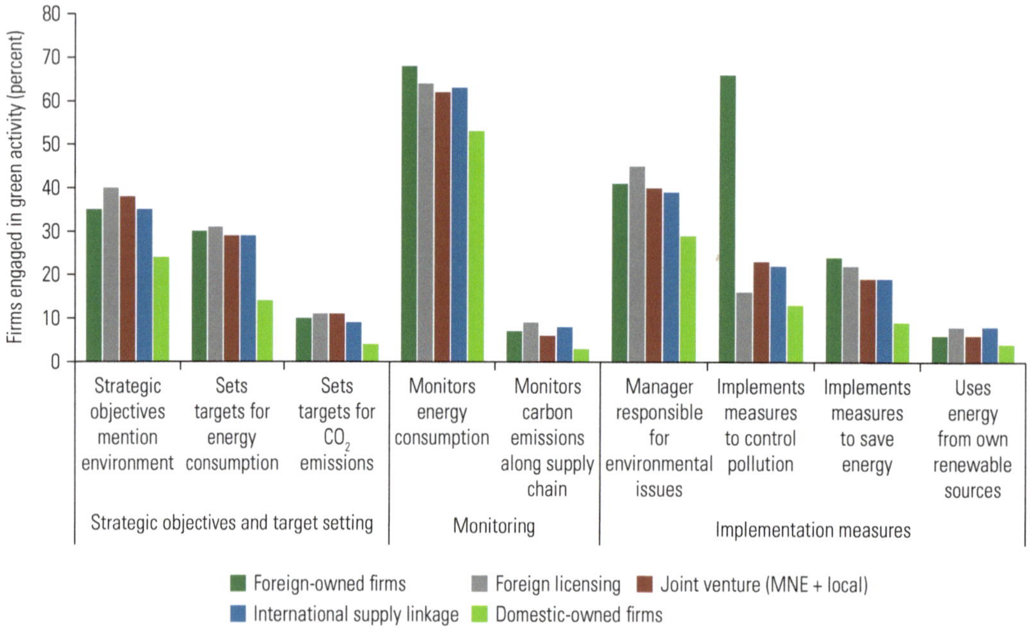

Source: World Bank calculations based on World Bank Enterprise Survey data 2020.

Note: CO_2 = carbon dioxide; MNE = multinational enterprise.

TABLE 3.1 The Role of Equity Alliances (Joint Ventures) and Green Performance of Firms

	Strategic objectives and target setting			Monitoring			Implementation measures		
	(1)	(2)	(3)	(4)	(5)	(6)	(7)	(8)	(9)
	Strategic objectives mention environment	Sets targets for energy consumption	Sets targets for CO_2 emissions	Monitors energy consumption	Monitors carbon emissions along supply chain	Manager responsible for environmental issues	Implemented measures to control pollution	Implemented measures to save energy	Used energy from own renewable sources
Joint venture	0.068***	0.077***	0.046***	0.080***	0.002	0.053***	0.039	0.033	0.011
	(0.023)	(0.028)	(0.014)	(0.029)	(0.013)	(0.019)	(0.024)	(0.030)	(0.013)
Foreign ownership	0.095***	0.031**	0.043***	0.052***	0.022***	0.081***	0.067***	0.049***	−0.011*
	(0.011)	(0.013)	(0.006)	(0.013)	(0.006)	(0.009)	(0.011)	(0.014)	(0.006)
Age	−0.000	−0.000	0.000	−0.000***	−0.000	−0.000	0.000	−0.000	0.000
	(0.000)	(0.000)	(0.000)	(0.000)	(0.000)	(0.000)	(0.000)	(0.000)	(0.000)
Large	0.188***	0.206***	0.074***	0.183***	0.059***	0.217***	0.178***	0.219***	0.052***
	(0.007)	(0.009)	(0.004)	(0.009)	(0.004)	(0.006)	(0.008)	(0.009)	(0.004)
Medium	0.072***	0.076***	0.021***	0.096***	0.018***	0.058***	0.070***	0.094***	0.023***
	(0.006)	(0.007)	(0.004)	(0.008)	(0.003)	(0.005)	(0.006)	(0.008)	(0.003)
Country FE	yes	yes	yes	yes	yes	yes	yes	yes	yes
Sector FE	yes	yes	yes	yes	yes	yes	yes	yes	yes
Year FE	yes	yes	yes	yes	yes	yes	yes	yes	yes
Observations	18,617	18,427	18,424	18,582	18,427	18,647	17,154	18,092	18,409

Source: World Bank calculations based on World Bank Enterprise Survey data.

Note: Robust standard errors in parentheses. Coefficients are marginal effects. CO_2 = carbon dioxide; FE = fixed effect.

* $p < 0.10$, ** $p < 0.05$, ***$p < 0.01$.

TABLE 3.2 The Effect of Supply Links on Green Performance of Firms

	Strategic objectives and target setting			Monitoring			Implementation measures		
	(1)	(2)	(3)	(4)	(5)	(6)	(7)	(8)	(9)
	Strategic objectives mention environment	Sets targets for energy consumption	Sets targets for CO_2 emissions	Monitors energy consumption	Monitors carbon emissions along supply chain	Manager responsible for environmental issues	Implemented measures to control pollution	Implemented measures to save energy	Used energy from own renewable sources
Supply links	0.089***	0.069***	0.034***	0.054***	0.039***	0.057***	0.068***	0.046***	0.038***
	(0.008)	(0.010)	(0.005)	(0.010)	(0.005)	(0.007)	(0.009)	(0.011)	(0.005)
Foreign ownership	0.092***	0.028**	0.041***	0.050***	0.021***	0.080***	0.066***	0.049***	–0.013**
	(0.011)	(0.013)	(0.006)	(0.013)	(0.006)	(0.009)	(0.011)	(0.014)	(0.006)
Age	–0.000	–0.000	–0.000	–0.000***	–0.000	–0.000	0.000	–0.000	0.000
	(0.000)	(0.000)	(0.000)	(0.000)	(0.000)	(0.000)	(0.000)	(0.000)	(0.000)
Large	0.180***	0.201***	0.072***	0.178***	0.055***	0.214***	0.173***	0.215***	0.048***
	(0.007)	(0.009)	(0.004)	(0.009)	(0.004)	(0.006)	(0.008)	(0.009)	(0.004)
Medium	0.069***	0.073***	0.019***	0.094***	0.015***	0.056***	0.068***	0.092***	0.021***
	(0.006)	(0.007)	(0.004)	(0.008)	(0.003)	(0.005)	(0.006)	(0.008)	(0.003)
Country FE	yes	yes	yes	yes	yes	Yes	yes	yes	yes
Sector FE	yes	yes	yes	yes	yes	Yes	yes	yes	yes
Year FE	yes	yes	yes	yes	yes	Yes	yes	yes	yes
Observations	18,399	18,217	18,222	18,364	18,220	18,429	16,975	178,90	18,201

Source: World Bank calculations based on World Bank Enterprise Survey data.

Note: Robust standard errors in parentheses. Coefficients are marginal effects. CO_2 = carbon dioxide; FE = fixed effect.

* $p < 0.10$, ** $p < 0.05$, *** $p < 0.01$.

the regression results on the role of international supply links (trade relations) on companies' environmental performance. This shows a significant and positive association between supply links and the nine green performance indicators, and their associations are all statistically significant at the 1 percent level. The positive role of supply links remains positive and significant after controlling for firm-level covariates and fixed effects including country fixed effects, sector fixed effects, and year fixed effects. Supply links have an especially strong impact on firms' adoption of strategic objective and target setting for energy consumption. Having an international supply link is associated with a 9 percentage point higher likelihood of incorporating environmental issues into a firm's strategic objectives, 5 percentage point increase in monitoring energy consumption, and 4–7 percentage point increase in implementing measures to control pollution, save energy or use energy from own renewable sources.

Foreign licensing has the strongest impact on a firm's implementation of measures to save energy. Table 3.3 shows a significant and positive association between foreign licensing and different dimensions of green performance indicators, suggesting that local firms with international licensing are more likely to adopt green technology than firms with no foreign licensing. These results are robust to specifications that include covariates and control for fixed effects. This suggest that firms with international licensing, for example, are on average 16 percentage points more likely to implement measures to save energy, 14 percentage points more likely to incorporate environmental or climate change issues into their strategic objectives, and 13 percentage points more likely to set targets for energy consumption.

All forms of MNE links can stimulate green performance, with technological licensing from foreign-owned companies having the most sizeable effects. Regression results of the effect of equity partnerships with foreign firms, technological licensing from foreign-owned companies, international supply links, and foreign ownership on the green performance of firms are presented in figure 3.4 (and table 3A.1 in annex 3A). The results suggest that all forms of links with MNEs have positive and significant impacts on green business practices of firms in the sample. Technological licensing with MNEs matters more in all three areas of green business practices (strategic objectives and target setting, monitoring, implementation measures) and their effects stand out in magnitude relative to other forms of MNE links. The associated coefficients are positive and are significant at 1 percent. International supply links also have an impact on firms' adoption of strategic objectives for climate change and target setting, monitoring, and implementation measures, but their coefficients are smaller. Finally, equity partnerships with foreign firms (joint ventures) have a large impact on firms' likelihood of incorporating climate change into their strategic objectives and their monitoring, but is not found to increase their implementation measures to improve their environmental performance.

TABLE 3.3 The Effect of Foreign Licensing on Green Performance of Firms

	Strategic objectives and target setting			Monitoring			Implementation measures		
	(1)	(2)	(3)	(4)	(5)	(6)	(7)	(8)	(9)
	Strategic objectives mention environment	Sets targets for energy consumption	Sets targets for CO_2 emissions	Monitors energy consumption	Monitors carbon emissions along supply chain	Manager responsible for environmental issues	Implemented measures to control pollution	Implemented measures to save energy	Used energy from own renewable sources
Foreign licensing	0.140***	0.132***	0.055***	0.087***	0.058***	0.117***	0.122***	0.161***	0.041***
	(0.007)	(0.009)	(0.005)	(0.009)	(0.004)	(0.006)	(0.008)	(0.010)	(0.004)
Foreign ownership	0.074***	0.010	0.034***	0.035***	0.014**	0.063***	0.050***	0.027*	−0.016***
	(0.011)	(0.013)	(0.006)	(0.013)	(0.006)	(0.009)	(0.011)	(0.014)	(0.006)
Age	−0.000	−0.000	0.000	−0.000***	−0.000	−0.000	−0.000	−0.000	0.000
	(0.000)	(0.000)	(0.000)	(0.000)	(0.000)	(0.000)	(0.000)	(0.000)	(0.000)
Large	0.168***	0.190***	0.068***	0.174***	0.050***	0.201***	0.162***	0.197***	0.046***
	(0.007)	(0.009)	(0.004)	(0.009)	(0.004)	(0.006)	(0.008)	(0.009)	(0.004)
Medium	0.063***	0.067***	0.018***	0.091***	0.013***	0.050***	0.062***	0.083***	0.020***
	(0.006)	(0.007)	(0.004)	(0.008)	(0.003)	(0.005)	(0.006)	(0.008)	(0.003)
Country FE	yes	yes	yes	yes	yes	yes	yes	yes	yes
Sector FE	yes	yes	yes	yes	yes	yes	yes	yes	yes
Year FE	yes	yes	yes	yes	yes	yes	yes	yes	yes
Observations	18,399	18,217	18,222	18,364	18,220	18,429	16,975	17,890	18,201

Source: World Bank calculations based on World Bank Enterprise Survey data.

Note: Robust standard errors in parentheses. Coefficients are marginal effects. CO_2 = carbon dioxide; FE = fixed effect.

* $p < 0.10$, ** $p < 0.05$, *** $p < 0.01$.

FIGURE 3.4 The Effect of MNE Links on Green Business Practices

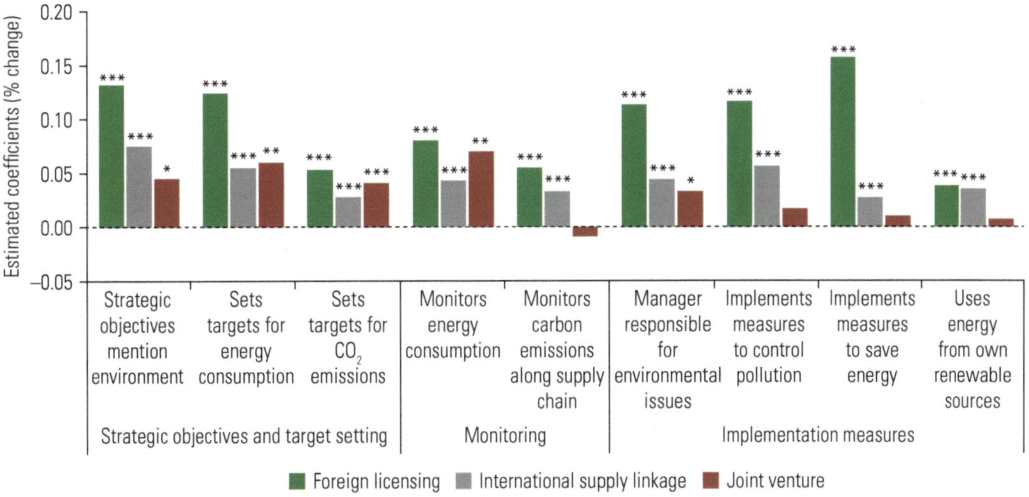

Source: World Bank calculations based on World Bank Enterprise Survey data.

Note: Results are from individual regressions, summarized in table 3A.1 in annex 3A. Each regression controls for country, sector, and year fixed effects as well as firm age and size. Parentheses report robust standard errors. Coefficients are described as marginal effects. CO_2 = carbon dioxide; MNE = multinational enterprise. * $p < 0.10$, ** $p < 0.05$, ***$p < 0.01$.

The Importance of Government Policy to Stimulate MNEs' Green Technology Transfers

Government and regulators have a fundamental role in driving the businesses toward sustainability. The primary rationale for such public policy interventions have been argued in the presence of market failures, for example when individual action does not account for externalities or when information problems impede desirable behaviors (Jaffe, Newell, and Stavins 2005; Pigato et al. 2020). Data from the World Bank's *Global Investment Competitiveness Report 2021/2022* (GIC) survey (World Bank, forthcoming) suggest that MNEs are particularly sensitive to such regulation. Government pressure is the most cited reason for investing in sustainable initiatives (by two-thirds of respondents; see table 3.4). For manufacturing MNEs, pressure from investors and disruption due to adverse weather events are key drivers as well. For information technology (IT)–enabled services and transport and logistics services MNEs, the role of pressure from customers is more prominent in shaping investment into sustainability measures.

The pressure exerted by governments and regulators can also encourage greater investments in sustainability initiatives (figure 3.5). The GIC survey 2021/22 also considered which firms were planning to increase their investment in four types of sustainability activities: (a) climate resilience, (b) use of renewable power and production decarbonization, (c) waste and non-CO_2 pollutions management, and (d) decarbonization

TABLE 3.4 Most-Cited Pressure to Become More Sustainable
Question: Did your company experience any of the following pressures with respect to sustainability in the past three years?

Sector	Most-cited	Second most cited	Third most cited
Automotive	Government pressure	Investor pressure	Disruptions/losses due to weather events
Food and beverages	Government pressure	Investor pressure	Disruptions/losses due to weather events
Textiles and apparel	Government pressure	Investor pressure	Customer pressure
IT and BPO	Government pressure	Customer pressure	None of these pressures
Transport and logistics	Government pressure	Customer pressure	Disruptions/losses due to weather events

Source: World Bank calculations based on GIC 2021/2022 survey data. (World Bank, forthcoming).

Note: BPO = business process outsourcing; GIC = Global Investment Competitiveness; IT = information technology.

FIGURE 3.5 Key Drivers for MNEs to Invest in Sustainability Initiatives
Question: Over the next 3 years, to what extent will your company invest in environmentally sustainable initiatives in developing countries, as compared to the past 3 years?

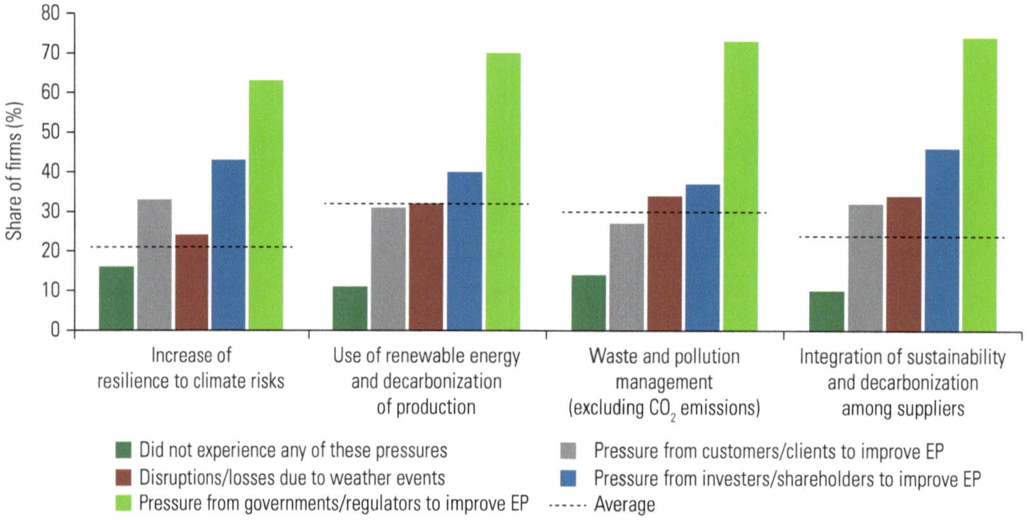

Source: World Bank calculations based on GIC 2021/2022 survey data (World Bank, forthcoming).

Note: This figure indicates the percentage of firms that is planning to increase their investment in environmentally sustainable initiatives. Number of observations = 1,060. CO_2 = carbon dioxide; EP = environmental performance; GIC = Global Investment Competitiveness; MNEs = multinational enterprises.

among suppliers. In each case, those who plan to invest were much more likely to have reported experiencing pressure from governments (63–74 percent of firms).

In sum, greater interaction with MNEs provides considerable potential for stimulating green technology transfers to developing countries. Foreign investment, the import of capital goods, and licensed deployment of technologies are all important channels of green technology transfers. Firms in developing countries linked to MNEs through

BOX 3.1 Future Research Agenda—Expanding Firm-Level Data on Climate Change Mitigation and Adaptation

This chapter draws extensively on the World Bank Enterprise Survey's Green Economy Module to consider the potential for green technology transfers. This survey provides valuable insights into firms' decisions on green strategic objectives and target setting, monitoring, and implementation measures. Yet, the data are available for only a few dozen countries, preventing more substantial analysis. Future advances in research relying on primary data at the firm-level and the Enterprise Survey could both expand geographical and topical coverage. For example, in addition to rolling out the Green Economy Module in more countries, the surveys should also sharpen the topical focus on climate change. This could include collecting information on the following:

- Strategies adopted by firms to raise environmental sustainability, such as management practices for production efficiency, resource use through circular economy practices, green innovation, adoption of clean technologies, and productivity and firm competitiveness
- Current challenges faced by firms related to climate change, and the potential technology and government policies that could help them to adapt and strengthen their resilience
- Investment needs and challenges faced by firms to adopt clean technologies and practices, lower their supply chain emissions, undertake process reengineering, and undertake other initiatives

Source: World Bank.

supply links, equity partnerships, or technological licensing arrangements are more likely to adopt green business practices, as compared to their peers without such links. Yet, in the presence of externalities and information asymmetries, MNEs are unlikely to investment an optimal amount in green technology or encourage their dissemination within their supply chains. Government pressure thus continues to be essential to encourage such green technology transfers, and is an important predicter of which MNEs will increase their investment in sustainability activities. Finally, to guide future research on green technology transfers, there is need for more firm-level data on climate change mitigation and adaptation (box 3.1).

Notes

1. A number of factors have been identified as drivers of technology transfer: absorptive capacity (Cirera and Maloney 2017), human capital and relevant technological skills and know-how (World Bank 2008), openness to trade and investment (Keller 2004; Popp 2011), market size (Keller 2004), and protection of intellectual property rights (Dechezleprêtre, Glachant, and Ménière 2012).
2. China for example, initially purchased turnkey production lines from German, Japanese, and US suppliers to build its solar photovoltaic industry. Imports contributed to the country's catch-up in production capabilities (de la Tour, Glachant, and Ménière 2011) and by 2008, China had emerged as the world's largest solar photovoltaic cell producer, accounting for more than one-third of global production.

References

Arnold, Jens Matthias, and Beata S. Javorcik. 2009."Gifted Kids or Pushy Parents? Foreign Direct Investment and Plant Productivity in Indonesia." *Journal of International Economics* 79 (1): 42–53.

Balaguer, J., A. Cuadros, and J. García-Quevedo. 2022. "Does Foreign Ownership Promote Environmental Protection? Evidence from Firm-Level Data." *Small Business Economics* (2022): 1–18.

Branstetter, L. G., R. Fisman, and C. F. Foley. 2006. "Do Stronger Intellectual Property Rights Increase International Technology Transfer? Empirical Evidence from U.S. Firm-Level Panel Data." *The Quarterly Journal of Economics* 121 (1): 321–58. https://doi.org/10.1162/003355306776083482.

Cirera, X., and W. F. Maloney. 2017. *The Innovation Paradox: Developing-Country Capabilities and the Unrealized Promise of Technological Catch-Up.* Washington, DC: World Bank. http://hdl.handle.net/10986/28341.

Dechezleprêtre, A., M. Glachant, I. Haščič, N. Johnstone, and Y. Ménière. 2011. "Invention and Transfer of Climate Change–Mitigation Technologies: A Global Analysis." *Review of Environmental Economics and Policy* 5 (1): 109–30. https://doi.org/10.1093/reep/req023.

Dechezleprêtre, A., M. Glachant, and Y. Ménière. 2012. "What Drives the International Transfer of Climate Change Mitigation Technologies? Empirical Evidence from Patent Data." *Environmental and Resource Economics* 54 (2): 161–78. https://doi.org/10.1007/s10640-012-9592-0.

de la Tour, A., M. Glachant, and Y. Ménière. 2011. "Innovation and International Technology Transfer: The Case of the Chinese Photovoltaic Industry." Energy Policy 39 (2): 761–70. https://doi.org/10.1016/j.enpol.2010.10.050.

Djankov, S., and B. Hoekman. 2000. "Foreign Investment and Productivity Growth in Czech Enterprises." *World Bank Economic Review* 14 (1): 49–64.

Glachant, M., D. Dussaux, Y. Ménière, and A. Dechezleprêtre. 2013. "Greening Global Value Chains: Innovation and the International Diffusion of Technologies and Knowledge." Policy Research Working Paper 6467, World Bank, Washington, DC. http://hdl.handle.net/10986/15600.

Jaffe, A. B., R. G. Newell, and R. N. Stavins. 2005. "A Tale of Two Market Failures: Technology and Environmental Policy." *Ecological Economics* 54 (2–3): 164–74. https://doi.org/10.1016/j.ecolecon.2004.12.027.

Keller, W. 2004. "International Technology Diffusion." *Journal of Economic Literature* 42 (3): 752–82. https://doi.org/10.1257/0022051042177685.

Lane, E. 2010. "Clean Tech Reality Check: Nine International Green Technology Transfer Deals Unhindered by Intellectual Property Rights." *Santa Clara High Technology Law Journal* 26 (4). https://digitalcommons.law.scu.edu/chtlj/vol26/iss4/2/.

Lewis, J. I. 2007. "Technology Acquisition and Innovation in the Developing World: Wind Turbine Development in China and India." *Studies in Comparative International Development* 42 (3–4): 208–32. https://doi.org/10.1007/s12116-007-9012-6.

Lovely, M., and D. Popp. 2011. "Trade, Technology, and the Environment: Does Access to Technology Promote Environmental Regulation?" *Journal of Environmental Economics and Management* 61 (1): 16–35. https://doi.org/10.1016/j.jeem.2010.08.003.

Mansfield, E., and A. Romeo. 1980. "Technology Transfer to Overseas Subsidiaries by U.S.-Based Firms." *Quarterly Journal of Economics* 95 (4): 737. https://doi.org/10.2307/1885489.

Mealy, P., and A. Teytelboym. 2020. "Economic Complexity and the Green Economy." *Research Policy* 51 (8). https://doi.org/10.1016/j.respol.2020.103948.

Pigato, M., S. J. Black, D. Dussaux, Z. Mao, M. McKenna, R. Rafaty, and S. Touboul. 2020. *Technology Transfer and Innovation for Low-Carbon Development.* International Development in Focus. Washington, DC: World Bank. http://hdl.handle.net/10986/33474.

Popp, D. 2011. "International Technology Transfer, Climate Change, and the Clean Development Mechanism." *Review of Environmental Economics and Policy* 5 (1): 131–52. https://doi.org/10.1093/reep/req018.

Rivera-Batiz, L. A., and P. M. Romer. 1991. "Economic Integration and Endogenous Growth." *Quarterly Journal of Economics* 106 (2): 531. https://doi.org/10.2307/2937946.

Ru, P., Q. Zhi, F. Zhang, X. Zhong, J. Li, and J. Su. 2012. "Behind the Development of Technology: The Transition of Innovation Modes in China's Wind Turbine Manufacturing Industry." *Energy Policy* 43: 58–69. https://doi.org/10.1016/j.enpol.2011.12.025.

Saggi, K. 1999. "Foreign Direct Investment, Licensing, and Incentives for Innovation." *Review of International Economics* 7 (4): 699–714. https://doi.org/10.1111/1467-9396.00194.

Saurav, Abhishek, and Ryan Chia Kuo. 2020. "Foreign Direct Investment and Productivity: A Literature Review of the Effects of FDI on Local Firm Productivity." FCI in Focus Working Paper, World Bank, Washington, DC.

Saurav, Abhishek, Peter Kusek, Ryan Kuo, and Brody Viney. 2021. "The Impact of COVID 19 on Foreign Investors: Evidence from the Quarterly Global Multinational Enterprise Pulse Survey for the First Quarter of 2021." World Bank, Washington, DC. https://openknowledge.worldbank.org/handle/10986/35803.

World Bank. 2008. *Global Economic Prospects 2008: Technology Diffusion in the Developing World.* Global Economic Prospects and the Developing Countries. Washington, DC: World Bank. http://hdl.handle.net/10986/6335.

World Bank. Forthcoming. *Global Investment Competitiveness Report 2021/2022: Examining the Potential of Foreign Investment in a Green, Resilient, and Inclusive Economic Recovery.* Washington, DC: World Bank.

Annex 3A. Additional Regression Tables on Determinants of Green Technology Transfers

TABLE 3A.1 Coefficients of the Three Main Types of Partnership and Foreign Ownership

	Strategic objectives and target setting			Monitoring			Implementation measures		
	(1)	(2)	(3)	(4)	(5)	(6)	(7)	(8)	(9)
	Strategic objectives mention environment	Sets targets for energy consumption	Sets targets for CO_2 emissions	Monitors energy consumption	Monitors carbon emissions along supply chain	Manager responsible for environmental issues	Implemented measures to control pollution	Implemented measures to save energy	Used energy from own renewable sources
Foreign licensing	0.132***	0.124***	0.053***	0.080***	0.055***	0.113***	0.116***	0.157***	0.038***
	(0.008)	(0.009)	(0.005)	(0.010)	(0.004)	(0.006)	(0.008)	(0.010)	(0.004)
Supply linkages	0.075***	0.055***	0.028***	0.043***	0.033***	0.044***	0.056***	0.027**	0.035***
	(0.008)	(0.010)	(0.005)	(0.010)	(0.005)	(0.007)	(0.009)	(0.011)	(0.005)
Joint venture	0.045*	0.060**	0.041***	0.070**	-0.009	0.033*	0.017	0.010	0.007
	(0.024)	(0.028)	(0.014)	(0.029)	(0.013)	(0.019)	(0.025)	(0.030)	(0.013)
Foreign ownership	0.075***	0.012	0.035***	0.038***	0.014**	0.065***	0.051***	0.029**	-0.018***
	(0.011)	(0.013)	(0.006)	(0.014)	(0.006)	(0.009)	(0.011)	(0.014)	(0.006)
Age	–0.000	–0.000	–0.000	–0.000***	–0.000*	–0.000	–0.000	–0.000	0.000
	(0.000)	(0.000)	(0.000)	(0.000)	(0.000)	(0.000)	(0.000)	(0.000)	(0.000)
Large	0.160***	0.183***	0.064***	0.166***	0.048***	0.197***	0.157***	0.193***	0.043***
	(0.007)	(0.009)	(0.004)	(0.009)	(0.004)	(0.006)	(0.008)	(0.010)	(0.004)
Medium	0.059***	0.064***	0.016***	0.088***	0.011***	0.048***	0.060***	0.082***	0.018***
	(0.006)	(0.007)	(0.004)	(0.008)	(0.003)	(0.005)	(0.006)	(0.008)	(0.003)
Observations	18,289	18,110	18,116	18,254	18,112	18,315	16,878	17,791	18,095

Source: World Bank calculations based on data from the World Bank Enterprise Survey 2020.

Note: Results are from individual regression. Each regression controls for country, sector, and year fixed effects as well as firm age and size. Robust standard errors in parentheses. Coefficients are described as marginal effects. CO_2 = carbon dioxide.

* $p < 0.10$, ** $p < 0.05$, *** $p < 0.01$.

4. How Committed Are MNEs Currently to Decarbonizing Their Supply Chains?

An essential prerequisite for countries to decarbonize their supply chains and to encourage green technology transfers to domestic firms is the active commitment of multinational enterprises (MNEs). As illustrated in the previous chapters, the supply chains of large MNEs make up the bulk of global emissions. To decarbonize such supply chains thus requires active engagement and investment by MNEs to shift out of high-carbon activities and shift toward more energy-efficient production methods. They will need to do this through capital upgrades and better management practices throughout the supply chain. It is therefore essential to consider how committed MNEs currently are to decarbonizing their supply chains.

MNEs are facing increased pressure to commit to more ambitious climate targets. Leaders of all major economies have pledged to take aggressive action to combat climate change. For example, the United States has pledged to reduce its emissions by 50 percent by 2030 from 2005 levels, while the European Union's green deal commits the bloc to climate neutrality by 2050. The implications of global coordination and policy actions will have significant impacts for companies across the world. Both the European Union and the United States are exploring the possibility of imposing a carbon border adjustment tax, which would apply to imports from countries with less ambitious climate policies. On top of that, MNEs are increasingly faced with pressure to commit to climate change reforms due to climate-conscious customers, environmental-, social-, and governance-guided (ESG) investors, and strict regulators. Jointly, this could shift the calculus for MNEs as they assess their business strategies.

More companies are signaling their intentions to take action on climate change. Based on analysis of nine reporting platforms by the NewClimate Institute and the Data-Driven Envirolab, as of October 2020, 1,565 companies, accounting for over US$12.5 trillion in revenue and 24.9 million employees, had set net-zero targets (NewClimate Institute and Data-Driven Envirolab 2020). These commitments have taken various forms—from comprehensive plans to reduce scope 1, 2, and 3 emissions to narrow goals for specific facilities or products, from concrete targets based on detailed tracking and reporting to general support for initiatives or pledges to soon develop the necessary action plans. Nonetheless, the combined carbon footprint of these companies amounts to 3.5 gigatons of annual emissions, greater than that of India

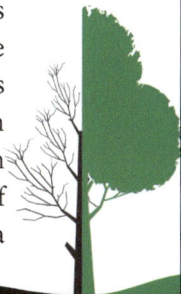

(NewClimate Institute and Data-Driven Envirolab 2020). Furthermore, by January 2022, the number of companies that made net-zero emissions pledges through the United Nations Framework Convention on Climate Change's Race to Zero campaign doubled from 2020, to over 3,000 (Day et al. 2022).

To analyze the commitments of MNEs in more detail, we again focus on 157 large MNEs—identified by Climate Action 100+—that jointly make up the bulk of global emissions. Climate Action 100+ offers detailed information on each MNE's commitments, for which it uses public and self-disclosed data from companies.[1] Companies are assessed against eight main indicators:

- Net-zero greenhouse gas (GHG) emissions by 2050 (or sooner) ambition
- Long-term (2036–50) GHG reduction targets
- Medium-term (2026–35) GHG reduction targets
- Short-term (up to 2025) GHG reduction targets
- Decarbonization strategy
- Capital allocation alignment
- Climate policy engagement
- Task Force on Climate-Related Financial Disclosures (TCFD)[2]

We use this to consider the commitments of MNEs based on their headquarters and also to consider a breakdown based on MNE affiliates using Bureau Van Dijk's Orbis database (see "Bottom-Up Approaches to Estimate the Effect of MNEs on Carbon Emissions" in chapter 2). We find that some MNE corporate boardrooms are devising measures to mitigate their effect on the climate and some of these changes hold considerable promise. But there is a real risk of a wide gap between ambitious plans and actual implementation—a type of greenwashing.[3]

MNEs' Commitments to Net-Zero Emissions by 2050

Less than a third of the world's most-emitting MNEs have formally established a commitment to have net-zero GHG emissions by 2050. Map 4.1 shows the commitment to net-zero GHG emissions by 2050 for the 157 large MNEs, based on the location of their headquarters. It then represents this as a share of all the large MNEs present in that country. This shows that there are eight countries where more than 75 percent of its largest MNEs have committed to net-zero emissions by 2050, all based in Europe.[4] Then, somewhere between 25 and 50 percent of large MNEs were committed to net-zero in another seven countries, either in Europe or East Asia. Most MNEs headquartered in other regions, such as Africa, North America, the Russian Federation, South America, or the rest of Asia are all still uncommitted to net-zero by 2050.

MNEs from high-income countries are more committed to the net-zero targets than developing countries, and MNEs in consumer goods and services sectors are more committed than those in transport, industrials, or energy sectors. Figure 4.1 shows that on average, only a quarter of all 157 large MNEs are committed to transitioning to

MAP 4.1 Share of MNEs Committed to Net-Zero GHG Emissions by 2050, by Headquarters Location

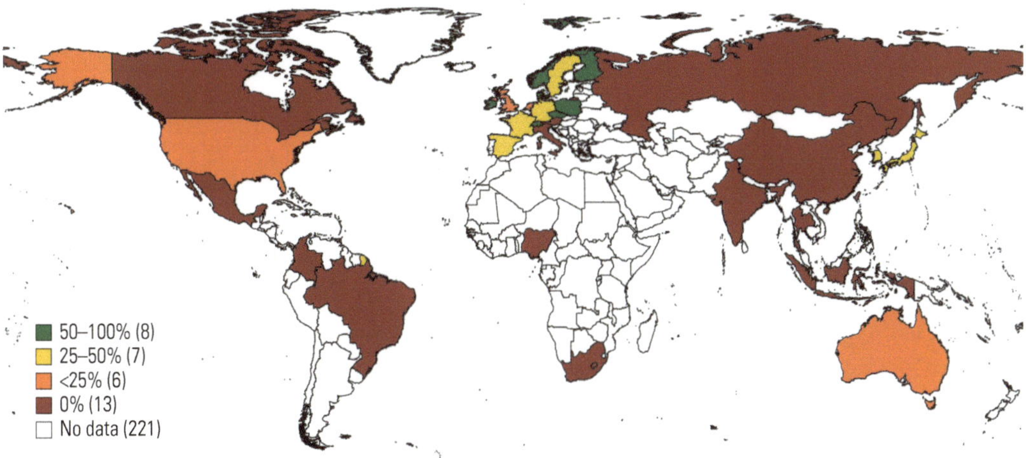

Source: World Bank calculations based on Climate Action 100+ data.

Note: The 157 companies are identified based on Climate Action 100+. Numbers in parentheses are the number of countries. GHG = greenhouse gas; MNE = multinational enterprise.

FIGURE 4.1 Large MNEs Committed to Net-Zero GHG Emissions by 2050, by Income Group and Sector

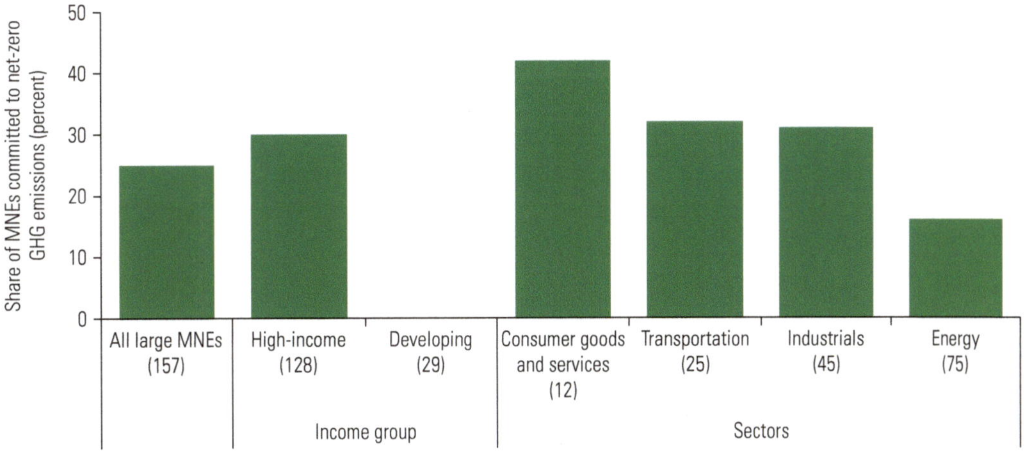

Source: World Bank calculations based on Climate Action 100+ data.

Note: 157 companies are identified based on Climate Action 100+. GHG = greenhouse gas; MNEs = multinational enterprises.

net-zero GHG emissions by 2050. Out of those, MNEs headquartered in high-income countries are more committed to net-zero targets (30 percent), while those headquartered in developing countries have none that formally committed. Yet the lagging nature of some large high-income countries (most notably Australia, Canada, and the United States, as shown in map 4.1) illustrates that many high-income countries still also face a considerable lack of MNE commitment. A sectoral breakdown shows that MNEs have higher commitments in the consumer goods and services sectors (42 percent), followed by transport (32 percent) and industrials (31 percent). Only 16 percent of MNEs in the energy sector were committed to a transition to net-zero GHG emissions by 2050—likely as this sector would face the most difficulty in their transition and in some cases it may be wholly unviable (for example, related to coal mining).

The Commitment of MNE Affiliates around the World

To better understand the potential risks and opportunities associated with the actions of large MNEs for climate change in specific countries, we need to consider their country-level importance for emissions together with their affiliates' commitment to reform. For this, the analysis makes use of Orbis and CDP's (formerly the Carbon Disclosure Project) Full GHG (Greenhouse Gas) Emissions Dataset to apportion each MNE's global emissions to their MNE affiliates (see "Bottom-Up Approaches to Estimate the Effect of MNEs on Carbon Emissions" in chapter 2 for details). From this, we identify the share of a country's emissions derived from these large MNEs' supply chains. Next, we consider the share of MNEs committed to a net-zero transition,[5] and weigh commitment based on their total emissions in the country. From this, we derive four quadrants (table 4.1 and map 4.2):

1. **High MNE emissions share, high MNE commitment.** In this case, these large MNEs are critical but also committed to change—thereby forming a significant opportunity to accelerate a country's emissions reduction. Policy makers could therefore collaborate with these large MNEs and see how to best realize their set-out objectives. This is the case in eight countries (concentrated in Europe).
2. **Low MNE emissions share, high MNE commitment.** Here, large MNEs are less critical as a source of emissions, but they are still committed—thus forming some opportunity for reform. Countries could leverage MNEs' goodwill to accelerate technology transfers that may help domestic firms decarbonize

TABLE 4.1 Categorizing Countries Based on the Emission Shares and Climate Commitment from Large MNEs

		Large MNEs' commitment to net-zero transition	
		High (>50%)	Low (<50%)
Share of emissions from large MNEs	High (>25%)	High MNE emissions share, high MNE commitment (8 countries)	High MNE emissions share, low MNE commitment (60 countries)
	Low (<25%)	Low MNE emissions share, high MNE commitment (25 countries)	Low MNE emissions share, low MNE commitment (43 countries)

Sources: World Bank calculations based on CDP, Climate Action 100+, OECD, and Orbis data.

Note: Considers the emissions-weighted share of firms that commit to net-zero emissions by 2050. CDP = formerly Carbon Disclosure Project; MNE = multinational enterprise; OECD = Organisation for Economic Co-operation and Development.

MAP 4.2 Country-Level Emissions Share and Commitments to Climate Action of 157 Large MNEs' Affiliates

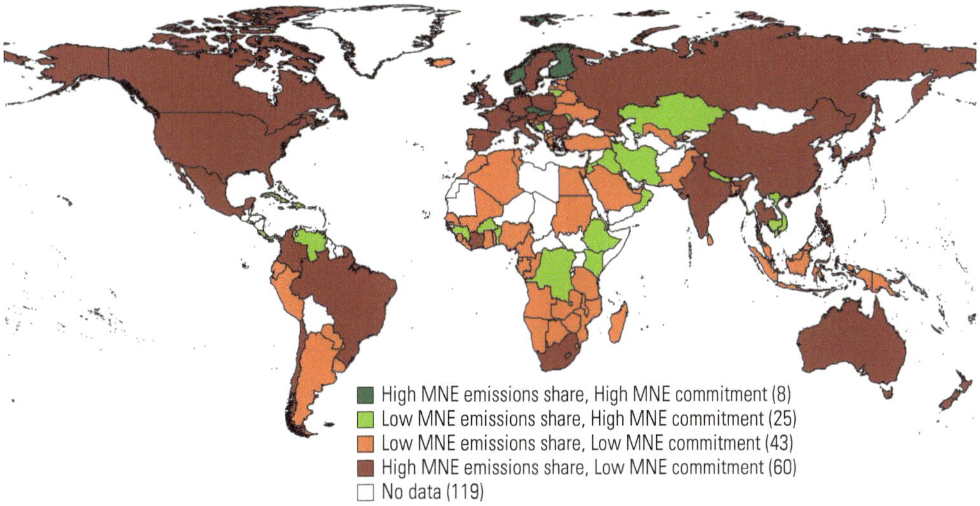

Sources: World Bank calculations based on CDP, Climate Action 100+, OECD, and Orbis data.

Note: Considers the emissions-weighted share of firms that commit to net-zero emissions by 2050. Numbers in parentheses are the number of countries. CDP = formerly Carbon Disclosure Project; MNE = multinational enterprise; OECD = Organisation for Economic Co-operation and Development.

their production. This is the case in 25 countries, present in Africa, Central Asia, Europe, and South America.

3. **Low MNE emissions share, low MNE commitment.** In this case, large MNEs are neither a very critical source of emissions, nor are they very committed. This presents some risk, as these polluting firms could lock the country into a high-emissions future. Yet given their limited role, there may be more urgent issues to focus on for climate mitigation. There are 43 countries where this is the case, spread across Africa, Central Asia, Europe, and Latin America.
4. **High MNE emissions share, low MNE commitment.** In this case, MNEs provide a significant risk to countries' climate change ambitions because they constitute a large share of emissions, but also display a weak commitment to reform. This suggests that policy makers would likely have to intervene more strongly to encourage these MNEs to sign up for more ambitious climate reforms to meet the country's own climate targets. Worryingly, this is the most prominent case, present in 60 countries, and includes some of the largest polluting countries around the world—most notably in Asia, Europe, and North America.

MNEs' Long-, Medium-, and Short-Term Strategies to Decarbonize

MNE headquarters' commitment quickly decreases as firms are asked to shift their long-term strategies into long-, medium- and short-term plans (figure 4.2, panel a).

FIGURE 4.2 **The Long-, Medium-, and Short-Term Commitment of 157 Large MNEs to Climate Action**

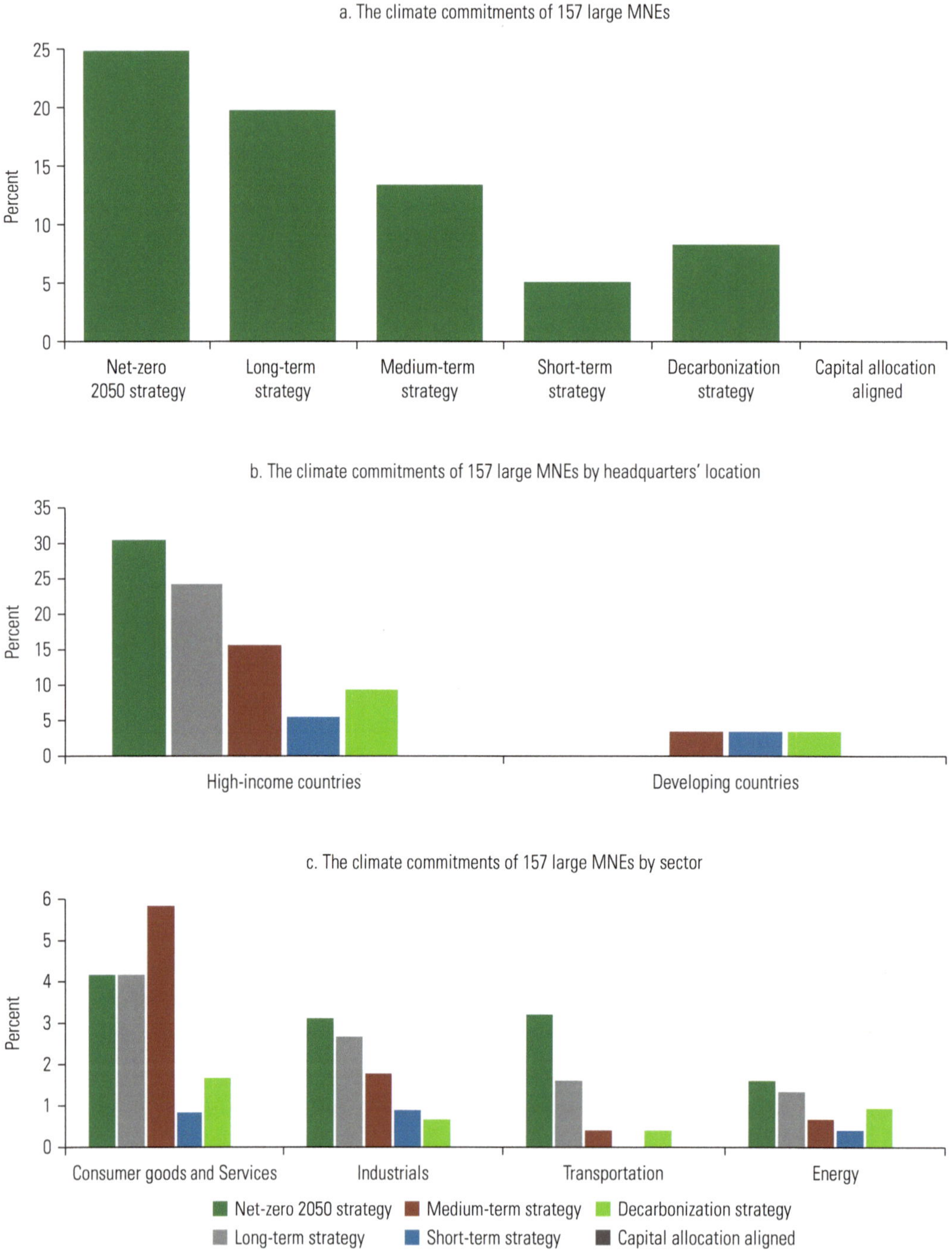

Sources: World Bank calculations based on data from Climate Action 100+ and Orbis.

Note: Long-term covers the period between 2036 and 2050, medium-term covers the period between 2026 and 2035, and short-term covers the period up to 2025. Sample size is 157 firms.

The previous section discussed the most long-term ambition—to ensure a company's broader supply chain has net-zero emissions by 2050. Yet, this is only the first step. It is equally critical for firms to translate ambitions into detailed long-, medium-, and short-term plans. Large MNEs are most likely to have a long-term ambition like net-zero GHG emissions by 2050. Yet, the share of firms with such targets quickly drops for having a long-term strategy (20 percent), a medium-term strategy (13 percent), short-term strategy (5 percent), or a decarbonization strategy (8 percent). None of the MNEs reviewed had a capital allocation strategy that was explicitly in line with a path toward net-zero emissions by 2050. Such gaps in long-term and short-term strategies do not bode well for climate action and suggest that MNEs' longer-term commitments are not supported adequately by shorter-term objectives. The lack of tangible plans to decarbonize production and supply chains in the short-term further raises credibility concerns about the realism of MNEs' long-term commitments.

When considering MNE affiliates, firms based in high-income countries are more likely to have plans in the long- and medium-term compared to those in developing economies (figure 4.2, panel b). MNEs headquartered in high-income countries are more committed to net-zero targets (30 percent), while none of the MNEs headquartered in developing countries have formally committed themselves to net-zero targets. Yet very few firms have a short-term strategy to reduce their emissions (6–7 percent) or a formal decarbonization strategy (4–10 percent). Yet the lagging nature of some big high-income countries (most notably Australia, Canada, and the United States—as shown in map 4.2) illustrates that many high-income countries still face a considerable lack of MNE commitment.

MNEs in the consumer goods and services sectors are considerably more likely to commit to climate action than in those in the industrials, transportation, or energy sectors (figure 4.2, panel c). Over 40 percent of MNEs in the consumer goods and services sectors have a net-zero strategy and long-term strategy, while almost 60 percent have a medium-term strategy in place. Just under 20 percent have a decarbonization strategy, which is considerably higher than any other sector. In contrast, both industrials and transportation sectors have much lower shares of medium-term strategies (18 and 4 percent, respectively) or short-term strategies (9 and 0 percent, respectively). The energy sector appears the least dedicated, with only 13 percent having any long-term strategy, 7 percent a medium-term strategy, and 4 percent a short-term strategy.

The differences among sectors are even starker when considering MNE affiliates—which also illustrates a distinction between high-income and developing countries (figure 4.2). Across all the 19,600 affiliates of the 157 MNEs, we see considerably higher commitment in the consumer goods and services sectors, where around 60–70 percent of MNE affiliates come from a company with a long- and medium-term strategy—for both high-income and developing countries. For industrials sectors, affiliates in

FIGURE 4.3 The Commitment of MNE Affiliates to Climate Action, by Sector

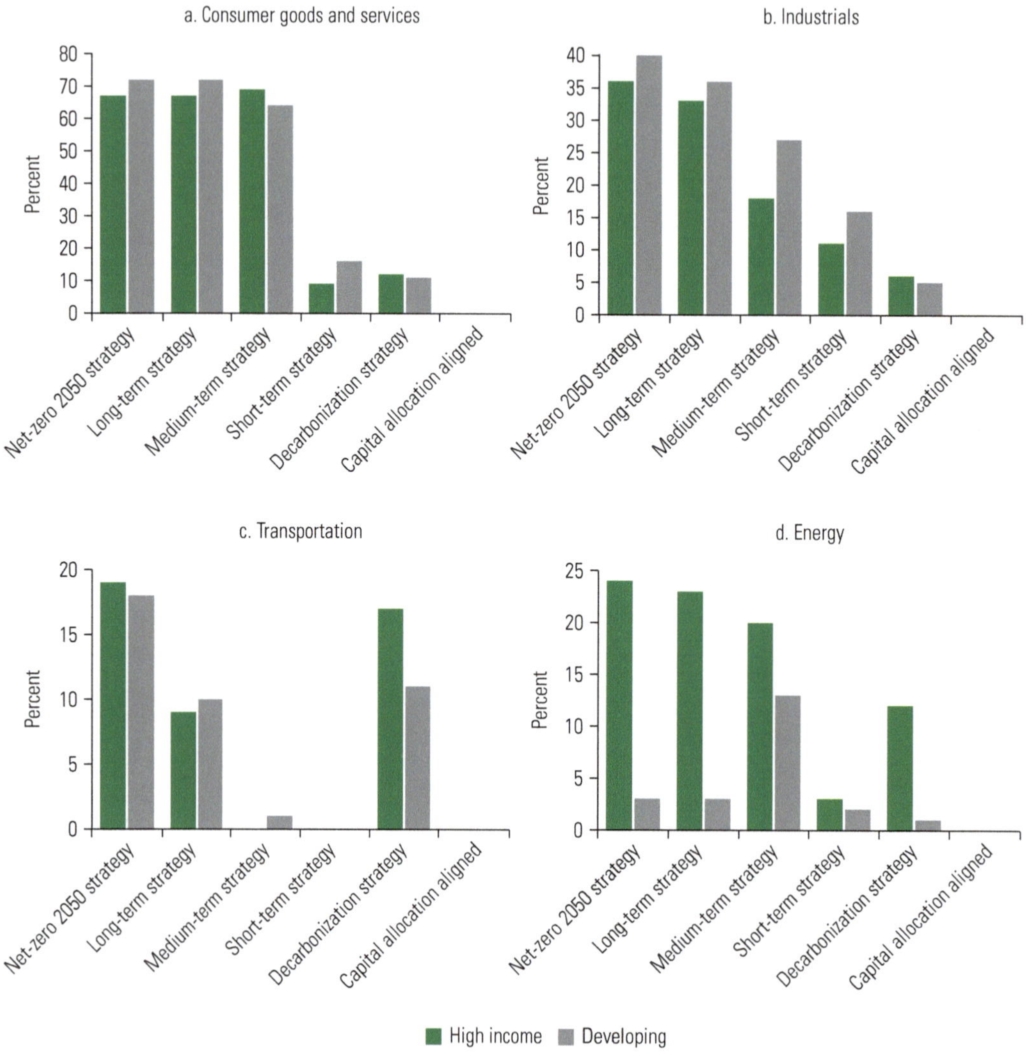

Sources: World Bank calculations based on data from the Climate Action 100+ and Orbis.

Note: Long-term covers the period between 2036 and 2050, medium-term covers the period between 2026 and 2035, and short-term covers the period up to 2025. Sample size is 157 firms. Sample size is 19,600 observations. The commitments of MNE affiliates are identified based on the MNE headquarters' commitment and assigned to all their subsidiaries. For this reason, panel b figures do not sum up to averages from panel a. MNE = multinational enterprise.

developing countries appear to have a higher commitment in the long, medium, and short run (36, 27, and 16 percent, respectively) than for high-income countries (33, 18, and 11 percent, respectively). In transportation sectors, some firms have long-term strategies (9–10 percent) and almost none have medium- or short-term strategies, but decarbonization strategies are more common (17 percent for high-income, and 11 percent for developing countries). Finally, the energy sector provides the biggest difference between MNE affiliates from high-income and developing countries for long-term strategy (23 versus 3 percent, respectively) and medium-term strategy (20 versus 13 percent, respectively). Both groups have very low rates of short-term strategies (3 and 2 percent, respectively).

Weaknesses in Corporate Climate Reporting and Greenwashing

New survey data suggest that a sizeable share of large MNEs track their greenhouse gas emissions, but also this is rarely independently verified or published. The World Bank's *Global Investment Competitiveness Report 2021/2022* (GIC) survey (World Bank, forthcoming) asked 1,060 large MNEs whether they track their GHG footprints across its foreign operations. As shown in figure 4.4, this shows that the majority of firms track their emissions globally across five sectors studied: automotives (69 percent), food and beverages (56 percent), IT-enabled services (77 percent), textiles (60 percent), and transport (61 percent). However, in each case, only a very small share of these large MNEs has independent verification and publication of their global GHG footprints. This is highest for IT-enabled services (37 percent) and automotives (22 percent), and between 10 and 14 percent for the other sectors. This lack of official monitoring and verification opens up the potential for underreporting or misreporting to governments and investors, and also limits the potential for any push to establish a formal program for MNEs to decarbonize their broader supply chain (for example, via investment or support to local firms).

FIGURE 4.4 **MNEs That Track Emissions, Independently Verify, or Publish, by Sector**
Question: Does your company track its greenhouse gas footprints across its foreign operations? Is the data independently verified and published?

- ■ Greenhouse gas footprints are tracked for all countries, and data are independently verified and published
- ■ Greenhouse gas footprints are tracked for all countries, but data are not independently verified or are not published
- ■ Greenhouse gas footprints are tracked for some countries ■ Greenhouse gas footprints are not tracked

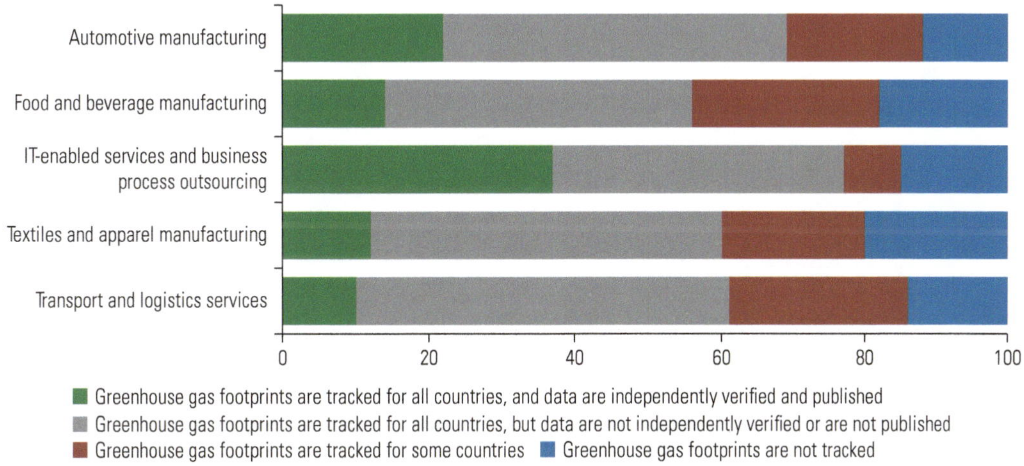

Source: World Bank calculations using GIC 2021/2022 survey data (World Bank, forthcoming).

Note: Number of observations = 1060. GIC = Global Investment Competitiveness; IT = information technology; MNEs = multinational enterprises.

Other examples confirm weaknesses in measurement and reporting for some of the largest and most visible MNEs in the world. The Corporate Climate Sustainability Monitor (CCSM) assesses the climate strategies of 25 major MNEs. Although all these companies have reported their emissions footprints on an annual basis, the report finds that only 7 of these 25 MNEs disclosed full details on all their scope 3 emissions sources—which account for 87 percent of total emissions for these companies, on average (Day et al. 2022). Related, fewer than half of these MNEs present any underlying activity data to complement their emissions disclosure. This level of detail in reporting is important for understanding emissions sources and the extent to which companies are taking steps to reduce their emissions.

Beyond monitoring, there are also weaknesses in how many MNEs set targets. The 25 MNEs covered in the CCSM all pledge zero-emission, net-zero, or carbon-neutrality targets. Yet only 3 firms commit to decarbonization of over 90 percent of their full value chain emissions by the target years of their headline pledges (Day et al. 2022). For 13 companies, the "net-zero" targets of these companies only commit them to reduce aggregate emissions from 2019 by around 40 percent, while another 5 companies commit to reducing their emissions by less than 15 percent. In most cases, these targets are thus deeply insufficient to achieve net-zero emissions, but firms purposefully omit either upstream or downstream activities to make up for the difference. Collectively, the 25 MNEs commit to reducing less than 20 percent of their emissions footprint—equivalent to 2.7 gigatons of CO_2—by their respective headline target years. As such, even firms who make explicit carbon commitments may fall short of meeting the targets set out in the Paris Agreement (Day et al. 2022). These observations hint at the deeper problem of companies intentionally given an overly flattering representation of their climate actions (greenwashing).

A first example of greenwashing is *cheap talk*—where companies show climate commitment via public relations initiatives rather than actual climate strategy and targets. For example, Bingler et al. (2022a) found that the establishment of the Task Force on Climate-related Financial Disclosures (TCFD) led to a 2.2 percentage point increase in the quantity of information disclosed between 2017 and 2020. Yet disclosure of information related to climate strategy, metrics, and targets increased negligibly and remained at comparatively low levels (Bingler et al. 2022a). Bingler and colleagues extended this analysis by constructing and analyzing a cheap talk index based on the ratio of nonspecific climate-related commitments to all climate-related commitments made by companies (Bingler et al. 2022b). Overall, their cheap talk index increased between 2010 and 2020.

A second example of greenwashing is purposeful misreporting. An example of this comes from Kim and Lyon (2011), who analyze the US Department of Energy's voluntary greenhouse gas disclosure registry and show that 68 percent of participants in the program reported significant reductions in GHG emissions despite their emissions having increased in reality. Meanwhile, companies that did not participate in the program actually reduced their emissions. The authors suggest that the program failed to significantly impact emissions intensity, in part because the program's reporting flexibility undermined its credibility (Kim and Lyon 2011). In a similar paper, Kim and Lyon (2015) also find that growing firms are relatively likely to overreport their emissions reductions. Although these studies focus on electrical utilities rather than MNEs, they indicate how strong the incentives for greenwashing are, especially in the presence of large information asymmetries.

Market Failures in Corporate Target Setting, Monitoring, and Reporting

The primary market failure impeding higher quality and more credible measurement, target setting, and reporting is imperfect information between firms and regulators and civil society. Firms are more informed than regulators and civil society about their emissions and hence about the validity of their emissions measurement and reporting. Firms may face an incentive to misrepresent their emissions performance to avoid reputational or other damage or to bolster their reputation and thus financial performance. In turn, the stock put into all firms' measurement, target setting, and reporting efforts may diminish as regulators and civil society struggle to differentiate honest firms from dishonest ones.

A range of factors is associated with higher or lower quality measurement and reporting by companies. These factors stem from the market (for example, consumer or investor demand), from nonmarket sources (for example, lax regulation, civil society monitoring), and from firm characteristics (Delmas and Burbano 2011).

The extent of external scrutiny appears to be particularly important in moderating inadequate or misleading reporting. For example, Kim and Lyon (2015) find that growing firms often overreport emissions reductions, but the extent to which they do so reduces by nearly two-thirds as external scrutiny increases. The same study analyzes how deregulation may lead to "brownwashing"[6]—the opposite of greenwashing due to pressure from investors to increase profitability in the absence of environmental regulations. This effect, however, is curtailed (though only to a small extent) by the presence of scrutiny from external stakeholders. Marquis, Toffel, and Zhou (2016) analyze 4,750 companies headquartered across 45 countries to explore the conditions under which companies causing significant environmental damage selectively disclose information about their environmental impacts. They find that companies are less likely to selectively disclose when there is a greater nongovernmental organization presence in their countries, and when they are located in countries that have more civil liberties and political rights.

External scrutiny may be more prevalent for large firms and for firms operating in environmentally damaging sectors, which may indicate their figures are more accurate than those in other sectors. Prado-Lorenzo et al. (2009) and Chithambo and Tauringana (2014) both analyze factors affecting emissions disclosure and find that firm size is positively associated with disclosure. From the sectoral perspective, Bingler et al. (2022a) argue that companies in the energy and utilities sector disclose the highest amount of climate-related information, and Bingler et al. (2022b) find that companies in the energy, industrials, materials, real estate, and utilities sectors engage in less cheap talk—with the strongest effect for those in energy and utilities. Analysis by Prado-Lorenzo et al. (2009) points to a similar set of sectors in which companies are more likely to disclose information on their emissions.

To limit corporate greenwashing requires more explicit initiatives to increase corporate disclosure of climate commitments and actions, greater standardization of emissions disclosure, and, ideally, oversight by third-party actors to oversee and validate climate target-setting and action. The authors of the cheap talk index review make three major recommendations (Bingler et al. 2022b). First, they show that engagement in initiatives by institutional investors like the Climate Action 100+ considerably increases the quality and decision-relevance of investees' disclosures of climate-related commitments and actions. Policy makers should empower these channels, for example, by protecting investor rights and encouraging the active engagement of institutional investors on climate-related topics. Second, they argue that voluntary emissions disclosures need additional standardization and guidance to ensure that the disclosed information and firms' commitments are materially relevant, useful for decision-making, and informative for investors and financial supervisors. Third, policy makers should encourage firms to rely on third-party actors to oversee and validate climate target-setting and action (Bingler et al. 2022b).

In sum, this chapter has reviewed the commitments of large MNEs to climate change reform. It finds that many MNEs are insufficiently committed to climate change reforms. Even the most long-term objective (committing to net-zero emissions by 2050) is lacking for a large share of them. This is especially the case in MNEs headquartered in developing countries, and for MNEs in the energy and transport sectors. When considering MNEs' commitments weighted by their country's emissions share, an even gloomier picture presents itself. Overall, we find that a large number of countries (60) have a very high share of MNE emissions (>25 percent and up) but few of their MNEs are currently explicitly committed to net-zero emissions by 2050. This poses a significant risk. Another major risk is that there is a significant disconnect between firms' long-term commitments and their short- and medium-term actions to get there. We find that that across all firms, this quickly tapers off, and very few have a meaningful short-term strategy. None of the 157 MNEs reviewed had their capital allocations aligned to an active climate transition. This mismatch suggests that MNEs may be engaged in greenwashing—that is, they are presenting more optimistic, long-term

BOX 4.1 Future Research Agenda—Monitoring MNEs' Climate Change Reform Commitments in Headquarters and Host Countries

To consider the climate commitments of multinational enterprises (MNEs), this chapter has mostly relied on the stated climate ambitions set out by MNEs' headquarters. It has also assumed that these ambitions apply entirely to the MNEs' broader affiliate structure. Going forward, this analysis can be improved in three ways:

- First, monitor the actual behavior of MNEs in closer detail and consider whether more ambitious climate commitments result in more active reforms or whether this is "cheap talk."
- Second, consider how MNE affiliates follow the climate ambitions and actions of their headquarters, as it is possible that the emissions commitment of MNE headquarters and MNE affiliates in foreign countries differ systematically.
- Third, with access to more granular data on climate change ambitions and actions, explore what may be driving these dynamics. Of particular importance would be to consider how environmental regulation in MNE headquarters as well as host countries may shape the actions of MNEs and their affiliates.

Source: World Bank.

strategies without adopting the required actions to implement them. Finally, we delve into the causes of greenwashing and suggest that this can be avoided through more explicit external scrutiny, greater standardization of emissions disclosure, and oversight by third-party actors to oversee and validate climate target-setting and action. Going forward, it will be critical to consider the climate ambitions and actions of MNEs and their affiliates, leading to an important research agenda (box 4.1).

Notes

1. Sources include company annual reports, sustainability reports, press releases, and CDP disclosures.
2. For more information, see https://www.climateaction100.org/.
3. For more on greenwashing, see "Weaknesses in Corporate Climate Reporting and Greenwashing" in this chapter.
4. These are the Czech Republic, Denmark, Finland, Ireland, Luxembourg, Norway, Poland, and Switzerland.
5. In this case, we assume that the emissions commitment of the MNE affiliate follows the ambitions set by the headquarters. However, going forward, it would also be important to monitor or review how host countries could shape the climate ambitions of MNE affiliates, to ensure they either match or exceed headquarters' targets.
6. "Brownwashing" refers to unduly *understating* corporate environmental activity (Kim and Lyon, 2015).

References

Bingler, J. A., M. Kraus, M. Leippold, and N. Webersinke. 2022a. "Cheap Talk and Cherry-Picking: What ClimateBert Has to Say on Corporate Climate Risk Disclosures." *Finance Research Letters* 47 (B). https://doi.org/10.1016/j.frl.2022.102776.

Bingler, J. A., M. Kraus, M. Leippold, and N. Webersinke. 2022b. "Cheap Talk in Corporate Climate Commitments: The Role of Active Institutional Ownership, Signaling, Materiality, and Sentiment." Swiss Finance Institute Research Paper No. 22-01. https://ideas.repec.org/p/chf/rpseri/rp2201.html.

CDP (formerly the Carbon Disclosure Project). 2022. *CDP Full GHG Emissions Dataset 2022: Summary*. CDP, London. https://www.cdp.net/en/investor/ghg-emissions-dataset.

Chithambo, L., and V. Tauringana. 2014. "Company Specific Determinants of Greenhouse Gases Disclosures." *Journal of Applied Accounting Research* 15 (3): 323–38. https://doi.org/10.1108/jaar-11-2013-0087.

Day, T., S. Mooldijk, S. Smit, E. Posada, F. Hans, H. Fearnehough, A. Kachi, C. Warnecke, T. Kuramochi, and N. Höhne. 2022. *Corporate Climate Responsibility Monitor 2022*. NewClimate Institute and Carbon Market Watch. https://newclimate.org/wp-content/uploads/2022/02/CorporateClimateResponsibilityMonitor2022.pdf.

Delmas, M. A., and V. C. Burbano. 2011. "The Drivers of Greenwashing." *California Management Review* 54 (1): 64–87. https://doi.org/10.1525/cmr.2011.54.1.64.

Kim, E.-H., and T. P. Lyon. 2011. "Strategic Environmental Disclosure: Evidence from the DOE's Voluntary Greenhouse Gas Registry." *Journal of Environmental Economics and Management* 61 (3): 311–26. https://doi.org/10.1016/j.jeem.2010.11.001.

Kim, E.-H., and T. P. Lyon. 2015. "Greenwash vs. Brownwash: Exaggeration and Undue Modesty in Corporate Sustainability Disclosure." *Organization Science* 26 (3): 705–23. https://doi.org/10.1287/orsc.2014.0949.

Marquis, C., M. W. Toffel, and Y. Zhou. 2016. "Scrutiny, Norms, and Selective Disclosure: A Global Study of Greenwashing." *Organization Science* 27 (2): 483–504. https://doi.org/10.1287/orsc.2015.1039.

NewClimate Institute and Data-Driven EnviroLab. 2020. "Navigating the Nuances of Net-Zero Targets." https://newclimate.org/wp-content/uploads/2020/10/NewClimate_NetZeroReport_October2020.pdf.

OECD (Organisation for Economic Co-operation and Development). 2022. *FDI Qualities Policy Toolkit*. Paris: OECD Publishing. https://doi.org/10.1787/7ba74100-en.

Prado-Lorenzo, J., L. Rodríguez-Domínguez, I. Gallego-Álvarez, and I. García-Sánchez. 2009. "Factors Influencing the Disclosure of Greenhouse Gas Emissions in Companies World-Wide." *Management Decision* 47 (7): 1133–157. https://doi.org/10.1108/00251740910978340.

World Bank. Forthcoming. *Global Investment Competitiveness Report 2021/2022: Examining the Potential of Foreign Investment in a Green, Resilient, and Inclusive Economic Recovery*. Washington, DC: World Bank.

5. Policies to Influence Multinational Enterprises' Effect on Climate Change

A host country's policy framework affects its investment climate, which in turn shapes the foreign direct investment (FDI) entering the country and its impact on carbon emissions. Policies to stimulate low-carbon investment are in some cases comparable to an enabling environment that is conducive to investment in general. Yet, conducive FDI policies will not automatically result in a substantial increase in low-carbon FDI or help decarbonization of supply chains (OECD 2022). Policy makers may also need to provide specific enabling conditions for low-carbon investments by developing policies and regulations that systematically internalize the cost of carbon emissions and facilitate low-carbon FDI and its knowledge and technology spillovers (OECD 2015).

The actions of multinational enterprises (MNEs) should play a central role in many countries' climate change mitigation strategies. As previous chapters have shown, MNEs could play a pivotal role in countries' climate change mitigation. A small number of MNEs influence a majority of global greenhouse gas (GHG) emissions through their supply chains. Yet, as leading actors, MNEs can also impose sustainability standards on their supply chains that, in some cases, would affect millions of producers (Thorlakson, de Zegher, and Lambin 2018). MNEs are more likely to use more advanced, low-carbon technology (see chapter 3), so their average carbon intensity is below that of domestic firms. MNEs also already face rising pressure from their shareholders to engage in lower-carbon activities (Bolton and Kacperczyk 2022). This presents an easier target (lower implementation cost to government) for either regulating or incentivizing environmental actions. This report also showed the significant potential that committed MNEs could provide for local firms in terms of green technology spillovers. Jointly, this provides a powerful argument for ensuring developing countries' policy frameworks actively seek to influence the actions of MNEs to accelerate the decarbonization of their local economy.

Policy makers can use a range of policy approaches (for example, the 5Ps) to help MNEs mitigate their impact on climate change and better stimulate green growth (figure 5.1). The 5Ps are patrolling (monitoring emissions), prescription (laws and regulations), penalties (taxes), payments (incentives and fiscal support), and persuasion (corporate commitments and information). These tools can encourage MNEs to reduce emissions-intensive production (scale), help MNEs shift their supply chains to

FIGURE 5.1 The 5Ps Framework: A Policy Approach to Influence MNEs' Effect on Climate Change

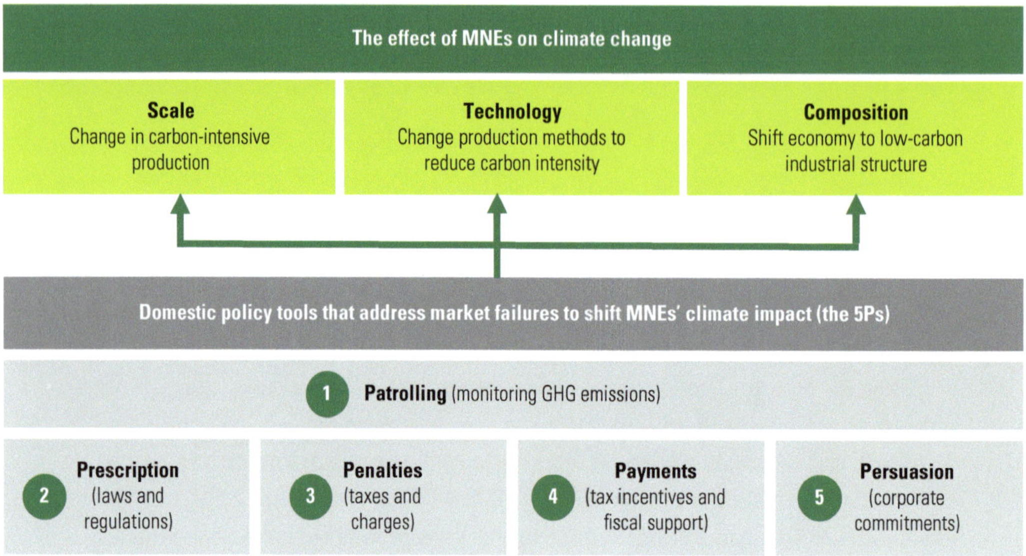

Sources: World Bank based on Grossman and Kruger 1991; Mandle et al. 2019.
Note: GHG = greenhouse gas; MNEs = multinational enterprises.

lower-carbon production methods (technology), and facilitate a shift toward a low-carbon industrial structure by attracting green FDI and phasing out dirty sectors (composition). Each approach has several policy instruments with which to affect the scale, technology, and composition channels of MNEs on climate change (table 5.1).

While the 5Ps instrument could be applied to all firms, large MNEs (and their supply chains) have specific characteristics that mean they may deserve special attention both through the choice of policy instruments and careful design of climate change policies. Two main elements set apart MNEs. First, their supply chain likely accounts for a disproportionate share of a country's emissions, so they will likely bear the brunt of most climate change policies (via any of the 5Ps). Second, MNEs often hold considerable bargaining power over host countries by being more unrestricted than domestic firms and threatening to shift their operations abroad (or to limit any future FDI). Jointly, this means that countries may want to pay special attention to MNEs in their policy framework, both through the choice of policy instruments and careful design to ensure the right balance so that MNEs (a) decarbonize their in-country supply chains; (b) collaborate more with domestic firms to encourage green transfers; and (c) do not feel so pressured that they choose to pull out of the country (and take with them particularly worthwhile capital, jobs, and technology).

The rest of this section will go through each of the 5Ps, illustrate which market failure or failures they seek to address, and elaborate on their advantages and disadvantages.

TABLE 5.1 Instruments to Improve MNEs' Effect on Climate Change (the 5Ps Framework)

Domestic policy tools	Objectives to improve MNEs' effect on climate change mitigation		
	Scale channel: Reduce carbon-intensive production	**Technology channel: Change in production methods to reduce carbon intensity**	**Composition channel: Shift economy toward a low-carbon industrial structure**
Patrolling (monitoring emissions)	• Monitoring firm-level GHG emissions (scope 1, scope 2, and scope 3) • Voluntary reporting standards and environmental disclosure laws		
Prescription (laws and regulations)	• Environmental standards • Emission permits	• Environmental standards • Streamlined regulations for technology licensing, joint ventures, local sourcing	• Restrictive business/FDI regulation for polluting sectors • Liberalized business/FDI regulation for green sectors
Penalties (taxes and charges)	• Environmental taxes	• Environmental taxes	• Higher income tax for polluting sectors
Payments (tax incentives, fiscal support)	• Buyout plans	• Incentives for green R&D, skills training, capital upgrades • Incentives for technology licensing, JVs, supplier programs	• Tax incentives for green sectors
Persuasion (corporate commitment, information campaigns)	• Corporate commitment campaigns	• Supply chain eco-certification • ESG/impact investing • Investor aftercare on green reinvestment and supplier links	• Green investment promotion and facilitation

Source: World Bank based on literature review.

Note: ESG = environmental, social, and governance; FDI = foreign direct investment; GHG = greenhouse gas; JVs = joint ventures; MNEs = multinational enterprises; R&D = research and development.

Particular emphasis will be given to the specific concerns associated with developing climate change policy for MNEs.

Patrolling (Monitoring Emissions)

Accurate monitoring of carbon emissions across all key domestic actors and supply chains is an essential start for policy makers to track and shape FDIs' effect on climate change. Monitoring is critical for key actors to help them understand that there is a problem and that it is in their interest to act. Transparency, based on the collection, disclosure, and wide dissemination of data and information on actors' practices, raises the visibility of the issue and can spur adoption of new green practices (Mandle et al. 2019). Supplementing this with more detailed firm-level surveys can provide policy makers with a valuable tool for self-assessment of FDI impacts on carbon emissions, and green growth more generally (OECD 2015). Without such information, policy makers may not know which firms are the biggest contributors to carbon emissions. MNEs, in turn, may also be unaware of their second- or third-tier suppliers, and this lack of knowledge may restrict their potential to encourage decarbonization across their supply chain.

Information itself can be a strong motivator to change behavior. Many firms (especially consumer-facing MNEs) go to great lengths to avoid bad publicity and preserve their reputations. Therefore, the more visible carbon emissions are made, the more likely firms are to shift their behavior (Thaler and Sunstein 2008). Information also helps makes public and private actors aware of unsustainable practices. For example, in China, a nonprofit organization created the China Water Pollution Map, a public database of information on pollution by factories in China, which spurred action both by government enforcement agencies and by the factories' customers (Gardner et al. 2018). Transparency can also play an important role in helping MNEs preempt disaster or respond more rapidly to crises. This is illustrated by the response of the apparel industry to the Rana Plaza accident,[1] or the response of food and agriculture companies to deforestation in the Amazon (Mandle et al. 2019).

The main market failure that impedes more credible measurement of carbon emissions is imperfect information between firms and regulators. Firms are more informed than regulators about their emissions and about the validity of their emissions reporting. They face an incentive to misrepresent their emissions performance to avoid reputational or other damage, or to bolster their reputation and thus financial performance (Kim and Lyon 2011). In turn, the stock put into all firms' measurement and reporting efforts may diminish as regulators struggle to differentiate honest firms from dishonest ones. Reporting standards, either voluntary or mandated, can help alleviate this market failure.

Voluntary reporting standards increasingly shape corporate monitoring of carbon emissions. The first major voluntary reporting standard was the Greenhouse Gas Protocol, launched in 1998, and it is the most widely used international protocol for measuring and reporting emissions. In 2016, about 92 percent of Fortune 500 companies employed the GHG Protocol, either directly or through a custom program based on the protocol. Brazil, India, Mexico, and the Philippines all employ GHG Protocol–based systems to collect valuable emissions data (UL Solutions 2020). The other international standard on corporate carbon reporting comes from the Task Force on Climate-Related Financial Disclosure (TCFD). This provides recommendations to companies on effective, clear, and consistent climate-related disclosure, including on the governance, strategy, management, and targets around climate-related risks. The TCFD is increasingly adopted by the largest carbon emitters and supported by the public sector (TCFD 2021). Companies often choose to adopt these measures to obtain a favorable environmental, social, and governance (ESG) rating[2] and convince investors that they are addressing the climate-related risks related to their operations and financial exposure.

Yet, voluntary reporting also comes with three major limitations. First, there are concerns about the accuracy of voluntary carbon disclosures. For example, for the US Department of Energy's voluntary GHG disclosure registry, 68 percent of participants reported significant reductions in GHG emissions despite their emissions having increased in reality (Kim and Lyon 2011). Second, companies also use these voluntary standards to greenwash their performance by intentionally emphasizing favorable climate actions rather than giving a more accurate—and perhaps less flattering—picture of their track record (Bingler et al. 2022). Third, providers of ESG ratings further exacerbate these issues by insufficiently reviewing and verifying firms' actual climate impact. Rating providers currently place the most weight on the disclosure of climate-related corporate policies and targets, with limited assessment as to the quality or impact of such strategies. Such limitations could mislead investors aiming to align portfolios with the low-carbon transition. Greater transparency and precision of climate-related corporate risks along the lines of the TCFD recommendations, for example, would facilitate investments into lower carbon assets (OECD 2022).

Environmental disclosure laws are critical to adequately capture the cross-border environmental footprint of MNEs. In acknowledging the limitations of voluntary reporting standards, countries are increasingly adopting mandatory emissions reporting (see box 5.1). In many cases, these requirements are restricted only to large companies. Yet such laws could incorporate emissions of smaller companies if large companies are required to monitor emissions for their whole supply chain. Going forward, mandatory emissions regulations are likely to have significant influence on the carbon implications of inward and outward FDI of companies around the world (OECD 2022). More developing countries should adopt these laws to accurately monitor carbon emissions across key actors and supply chains.

Prescription (Laws and Regulations)

Prescription (laws and regulations) shapes the behavior of MNEs and domestic firms alike. Environmental performance standards, such as emissions standards, restrict the emissions or energy use of vehicles, power plants, buildings, appliances, and industrial processes. For example, fuel economy standards apply to the fuel efficiency of new road vehicles, while emissions standards of power plants regulate the carbon intensity of their electricity mix (OECD 2022).

Environmental regulations and standards are widespread, but there are active debates about their efficiency. Prescriptive regulations are the most direct and most common form of environmental law. Yet, they are often criticized as inefficient and unwieldly. Regulation is thought to provide little incentive for innovation because once regulated parties satisfy the necessary requirement, the law creates no incentive to reduce harmful activities further (Mandle et al. 2019). As such, price-based instruments (such as taxes) are often argued to be preferable to regulatory standards (Baumol and Oates 1988; Harrington, Morgenstern, and Nelson 1999).

BOX 5.1 Mandatory Emissions Reporting around the World

At least 40 countries require companies to measure and report their emissions periodically (including most Group of 20 countries, G20). Policy makers use these data to inform their environmental policy decisions and track progress.

The United States

- Since 2009, the United States has required facilities emitting at least 25,000 metric tons or more of carbon-dioxide equivalent (CO_2e) per year to report their greenhouse (GHG) emissions to the Environmental Protection Agency (EPA). Jointly, these large firms cover around half of total US emissions.
- California has been requiring GHG emissions reporting since 2006, under the California Global Warming Solutions Act. The threshold for reporting in California is 10,000 metric tons of CO_2e, so businesses that do not meet the EPA's threshold may still have to report their emissions to the California Air Resources Board.

European Union

- Since 2014, the European Union (EU) has required public-interest companies, such as banks and insurance companies, with 500 or more employees to report on their environmental and social impact under the Non-Financial Reporting Directive. Jointly, this covers around 6,000 EU companies.
- The EU Taxonomy Regulation became law in 2020, placing a reporting obligation on companies with 500 or more employees to disclose how much of their global investment aligns with green and polluting activities.

Australia

- Since 2007, Australia has had mandatory emissions reporting under the National Greenhouse and Energy Reporting Scheme. Only companies that meet certain emissions thresholds are required to report. Companies use an online tool called the Emissions and Energy Reporting System to report their data.

South Africa

- In 2016, South Africa introduced the National Greenhouse Gas Emission Reporting Regulations. This program requires corporations across a set of high-emitting sectors, and which meet certain thresholds, to register and report their emissions to the Department of Environmental Affairs.

Sources: UL Solutions 2020; OECD 2022.

However, in the presence of specific market failures, regulations may be preferable to price-based instruments. For example, emission intensity standards can be preferable to emission taxes in sectors where production has positive external consequences (for example, knowledge creation, transportation), because they generally have less of an impact on output (World Bank 2012). Emission intensity standards can also improve social welfare relative to emission taxes in the presence of market power (Holland 2009). The idea that a unique carbon price in the economy is the optimal policy has been challenged in situations in which future carbon prices are unpredictable (Vogt-Schilb and Hallegatte 2011); technologies exhibit lock-ins, making it difficult to disseminate new technological options (Kalkuhl, Edenhofer, and Lessmann 2011); or labor markets or revenue-raising taxes are distortionary (Richter and Schneider 2003).

When enforcement costs are factored in, regulatory approaches may often be the easiest and most efficient solutions to reduce the carbon intensity of MNE production. Introducing a new standard may prove easier than price-based instruments, especially in sectors that are already regulated. In such cases, existing institutions can be relied upon to enforce new norms, and complex policy making may not be necessary (World Bank 2012). Prescriptive regulation can also be very effective in mandating uniform compliance across all actors, preventing problems of holdouts, free riders, and collective action (Mandle et al. 2019). Environmental standards may thus be effective to reduce the carbon intensity of production.

Many developing countries are unnecessarily worried that adopting more stringent environmental regulation would deter their attraction of FDI. Box 5.2 looks into this pollution haven hypothesis in more detail. There is no systematic evidence that investors' locational decisions are driven by differences in stringency of environmental regulations. Moreover, the rise of global carbon border policies such as the European Union's (EU) Carbon Border Adjustment Mechanism counters any incentives for MNEs to engage in "carbon leakage," that is, moving production from a country with stringent environmental policies to a country that is more lenient (Brenton and Chemutai 2021). Instead, higher environmental standards are expected by final consumers and product regulators, so robust environmental regulation may increasingly become a prerequisite to attract FDI and core to countries' value proposition to investors (Saurav and Viney 2021).

In some cases, environmental regulations have also been leveraged to explicitly target MNEs and accelerate the decarbonization of their supply chains. There is a growing demand in high-income countries to hold multinationals accountable for their climate impact. In some cases, this has led civil society organizations to pursue legal action. For example, in May 2021, a Dutch court ruled that Royal Dutch Shell (Shell) must reduce its aggregate CO_2 emissions (scope 1, 2, and 3) by 45 percent by 2030 (compared to 2019), regardless of the policies of the Dutch government. The ruling asserts that CO_2 emissions associated with Shell's supply chain breaches the company's legal obligation to prevent climate change. It also emphasizes that Shell's headquarters has responsibility over the entire Shell group, including all its subsidiaries. Such rulings thus suggest that environmental regulation can be extremely powerful in shaping the obligations of companies to prevent environmental damage (Wilde-Ramsing, de Leth, and Wolfkamp 2021).

BOX 5.2 Does Environmental Regulation Hurt Host Countries' FDI Inflows?

Many developing countries are worried about adopting more stringent environmental policies because of the concern that this would deter foreign investors from establishing there. This theory, also known as the "pollution haven hypothesis," posits that the costs imposed by environmental policies can drive firms to relocate economic activity, causing industries with a significant environmental footprint to shift production from well-regulated developed economies to less restrictive developing economies (Cole 2004; Copeland and Taylor 1994).

There is no systematic evidence that investors' locational decisions are driven by differences in stringency of environmental standards and regulations (Saurav and Viney 2021). While some empirical studies have linked historical foreign direct investment (FDI) inflows to higher carbon emissions in developing countries (Omri, Nguyen, and Rault 2014; Shahbaz et al. 2015), the environmental regulations in countries generally play little to no role in the investment and production decisions of most multinational enterprises (MNEs) (Koźluk and Timiliotis 2016).

Emerging evidence suggests that robust and stable environmental regulations may even contribute to attracting and retaining FDI flows. Adopting regulations and standards that reinforce climate goals can help level the playing field for foreign investments in low-carbon technologies, services, and infrastructure (OECD 2022). Some MNEs with strong corporate social responsibility mandates are shown to avoid investing in countries with weak environmental regulations (Dam and Scholtens 2008; Poelhekke and van der Ploeg 2015), leading some to find a positive effect of environmental regulation on inward FDI flows (Kim and Rhee 2019; Rivera and Oh 2013).

Finally, while there are anecdotal examples of the pollution haven for emissions-intensive activities, the rise of global carbon border policies drastically counters any incentives for MNEs to engage in "carbon leakage." It may still be tempting for some MNEs to relocate their most emissions-intensive activities to countries with weak environmental regulations. For example, Borghesi, Franco, and Marin (2020) found that the European Union's (EU) Emissions Trading System had some effect in raising outward investment and shifting production from Italian automotive companies to their subsidiaries abroad. However, new initiatives such as the EU's Carbon Border Adjustment Mechanism make it increasingly costly to import from countries with weak regulatory environments, thereby defeating the purpose of such carbon leakage (Brenton and Chemutai 2021). As such, it is expected that weak regulations are increasingly irrelevant as a measure of FDI competitiveness, even for the most polluting industries.

Source: World Bank based on Saurav and Viney 2021.

In designing environmental regulations, care should be given to minimize the costs for existing and new businesses. Policy makers must be careful to design environmental regulation in a way that does not create additional barriers for firms to enter markets, but instead creates incentives for innovation as firms seek to meet higher standards at the lowest possible cost (Saurav and Viney 2021; World Bank 2012). Copeland (2012) finds that environmental standards often favor incumbent firms at the expense of new entrants, thereby reducing the ability of the economy to innovate and grow. Yet several studies show that there can be a positive relationship between environmental regulation and innovation. This either focuses on the impact on innovation within existing firms (Ambec et al. 2011; Cohen and Tubb 2018) or showcases how new businesses help countries shift to more sustainable products and practices (Gast, Gundolf, and Cesinger 2017; Haldar 2019; Johnson and Schaltegger 2019).

In some cases, streamlining business regulations can ease compliance and administrative costs without reducing protections. In many countries there is scope to reform compliance processes and requirements while maintaining or even enhancing the overall level of environmental protections that are in place (Berestycki and Dechezlepêtre 2020; Koźluk 2014). Reducing the compliance-cost burden of regulation can be done in many ways, including creating integrated, digital systems; simplifying processes; enhancing transparency for firms; and prioritizing regulatory supervision based on risk. To illustrate, Saurav and Viney (2021) use the example of environmental licensing in Brazil's Ceára state. By simplifying licensing for low-risk firms, this reform eased the regulatory burden of the private sector and freed up scarce resources within the environmental agency to focus on more impactful oversight activities.

Liberalizing regulation could also provide opportunities for both business and the environment. Examples of this include the following: removal of sectoral restrictions may allow companies to better manage their environmental impact; new mechanisms for natural resource governance may create business opportunities in ecosystem management; and integrated licensing and permitting processes may better ensure overall enforcement of standards (Ploeg, Hinojosa, and Miedzinski 2017). Other examples relate to the streamlining of regulations that facilitate or encourage the relationships between MNEs and domestic firms (such as technology licensing, joint ventures, or local sourcing). Regulatory reforms that make this easier could encourage green technology transfers.

Finally, the legal rules and regulations governing the entry and operation of FDI also critically shape the various opportunities to attract and retain sustainable investment. The rules governing FDI and associated investment policies are a critical element of a country's investment climate. Excessive screening and restrictions (on ownership, products, technologies, and prices) can deter FDI, whereas strategic and focused investment promotion activities can help countries attract and retain FDI in key sectors. In turn, FDI can play a significant role as a source of finance for new projects and businesses, and as a mechanism to accelerate productivity growth by transferring knowledge and technologies to host economies (Kusek, Saurav, and Kuo 2020). Policy makers can therefore shape the composition of their economy by choosing to liberalize their business and FDI regulations for green sectors. They could even go one step further and adopt more stringent FDI regulations for dirty sectors, which would prevent them from being locked into a carbon intensive industrial structure.

Penalties (Taxes and Charges)

Another approach to limit the polluting activities of MNEs (or firms more broadly) is to ensure that price signals reflect the environmental costs of emissions. This enables polluters to internalize the negative externalities of their behavior. Environmental taxes are any taxes whose base "is a physical unit (or a proxy of it) that has a proven specific negative impact on the environment."[3] Taxes can include those on energy, transportation, pollution, and resources. These taxes leverage price signals to discourage the burning of fossil fuels and other environmentally damaging activities while promoting innovation and investment in cleaner, more efficient sources of energy (Pigato 2019).

Environmental taxes are gaining popularity as an effective way to address overinvestment in carbon-intensive activities. Such taxes can minimize the economic costs (or raise economic activity) of cutting pollution across different firms and industries in the economy by realigning price incentives (OECD 2022). They are especially useful for addressing large-scale global pollutants with multiple sources, such as carbon dioxide. Environmental taxes may also be especially important for developing countries with large informal sectors. Environmental taxes can be imposed on a small number of energy importers and major polluters in the country (many of which may be MNEs), who pass on the cost to other economic players. In contrast, the informal sector would likely evade any environmental standards regulatory restrictions placed on them. For other environmental externalities, direct regulations may be more pragmatic and cost-effective, especially when the revenues from taxation would be low and the costs of administering market-based instruments would be high (see "Prescription [Laws and Regulations]" in this chapter) (Pigato 2019).

The benefits of environmental taxes could also extend beyond environmental goals. Environmental taxes can often raise domestic revenues at a lower cost than other taxes because they tax a broad base (including the informal sector) and are relatively easily administered (OECD 2015). The revenues produced by such taxes can also finance investment in climate change mitigation and adaptation, offset the social impact of other forms of pollution, and accelerate the transition to more efficient infrastructure and cleaner technologies. These co-benefits are particularly large in developing countries and often justify the use of environmental taxes even before climate change mitigation benefits are considered (Pigato 2019).

A first concern with pricing policy is that the resulting outcomes may be regressive. While wealthier households may bear a larger absolute amount of total environmental taxation, policy makers may be concerned that the costs borne by the poor may represent a greater share of their household income. However, taxes on hydrocarbon fuels are generally progressive in developing countries as poorer households spend a smaller share of their income on pollution-intensive goods (such as automobiles and electricity) (Parry, Mylonas, and Vernon 2017). At the same time, the welfare costs of environmental externalities, such as ill health due to local air pollution, are heavily concentrated among the poor. As such, environmental taxes could promote shared prosperity.

Environmental taxes can also be made progressive by directly compensating lower-income households. When price increases do affect the types of goods purchased by low-income households, compensation will be important. This is surprisingly affordable. Dinan (2015) finds that in developed countries, 6 to 12 percent of the revenue from a carbon tax would be sufficient to compensate households in the lowest income quintile. In developing countries, where environmental taxation tends to be more progressive, compensating poorer households would likely require a smaller share of revenues (Pigato 2019).[4]

A second concern for policy makers is the potential impact on a country's competitiveness (similar to the issue raised on environmental laws). Environmental taxation may raise the production costs of companies and make it harder to compete internationally, especially in energy-intensive tradable sectors. If such taxes are adopted unilaterally, this may push some MNEs to relocate production to countries with lower environmental tax rates (similar to the pollution haven hypothesis discussed in "Prescription [Laws and Regulations]" in this chapter). However, energy represents a relatively small share of production costs in most (but not all) industries, and so the average adverse competitiveness effects tend to be small.

Most of the concerns are concentrated in a few energy-intensive and trade-exposed sectors. For these sectors, the issues are more salient. Box 5.3 reviews some evidence on the effect that environmental taxes may have on firm performance, considering the cases of Indonesia and Mexico. This suggests that complementary interventions in renewable energy may be necessary to maintain the competitiveness of large firms (including MNEs) and ensure adequate access to low-cost electricity (Pigato 2019).

Payments (Tax Incentives, Fiscal Support)

Policy makers can also use direct payments to firms to encourage specific behaviors. In the same way that governments can shift the price signals for firms to capture negative externalities and make bad activities more expensive, it can also use payments (such as tax incentives or direct subsidies) to capture positive externalities and make socially desirable activities less expensive (Mandle et al. 2019).

Subsidies can be justified if the positive externalities generated compensate for their present social cost. Many governments offer tax concessions or subsidies with the goal of steering investment into preferred sectors or specific regions or to raise the developmental effects of investments (James 2013). These types of subsidies can be justified if they generate positive externalities that compensate the present social costs of these

BOX 5.3 **How Do Environmental Taxes Affect Productivity and Competitiveness in Developing Economies?**

To consider the effect of environmental taxes on firm performance, Pigato (2019) conducts country-specific analyses using panel data for manufacturing plants in two developing economies that have highly subsidized fuel prices—Indonesia (1990–2015) and Mexico (2009–15). These analyses evaluate how changes in energy prices, particularly electricity and fuel, affect the behavior of plants across different regions and sectors. Interestingly, the findings suggest that increases in energy prices can improve firms' performance.

In Indonesia and Mexico, higher energy prices improved plant-level performance, a result driven entirely by fuel prices. This surprising result is explained by firms' adopting more productive and energy-efficient capital in response to fuel price hikes. Fuel price increases incentivized plants' purchase of new machinery and scrapping of old, fuel-based machinery. Plants became more energy efficient and used more electricity in response to fuel price increases, consistent with changes in the technical efficiency of production. Performance is less affected by fuel price increases in larger and foreign-owned firms, consistent with the idea that these firms operate closer to the technological frontier than do small, domestic firms, and therefore have less room to adopt new machinery.

The study does find that the price of electricity is negatively related to performance in both countries. The negative effects of electricity price increases on performance are consistent with the idea that electricity-powered machines tend to be closer to the efficiency frontier than fuel-powered machines and hence the price increase reduces their performance.

These findings provide reason for optimism and caution. The evidence supports the Porter hypothesis (Ambec et al. 2011), which holds that stringent environmental taxes can result in innovation by enabling companies to improve productivity, thereby more than offsetting compliance costs. However, these benefits appear to be mostly concentrated in smaller domestic firms. In contrast, there may be some concern that environmental taxes can hurt the competitiveness of multinational enterprises in energy-intensive sectors. This suggests complementary interventions in renewable energy may be necessary to ensure adequate access to low-cost electricity.

Source: Pigato 2019.

subsidies (Harrison and Rodríguez-Clare 2009; Margalioth 2003; Wade 1990). For green subsidies, different justifications used by policy makers affect either the scale, technology, or composition channels of firms' effect on climate change:

- Compensating firms for avoiding future pollution with buyout plans (scale)
- Subsidizing green innovation by strengthening research and development (R&D) initiatives (technology)
- Subsidizing MNE-links programs to stimulate green technology transfers (technology)
- Providing incentives to attract FDI in green sectors (composition)

A first—and perhaps somewhat usual—way that governments could use payments to reduce their emissions is to engage in buyout plans for dirty sectors, such as coal.

Retiring existing coal power plants before they complete their life cycle can be a rapid way for countries to reduce their carbon emissions. An example of this comes from the Netherlands, which provided a €200 million payout to shut down a privately operated 731-megawatt coal plant (Franke 2021). The Asian Development Bank (ADB) has also introduced proposals to buy and retire coal plants across Bangladesh, Indonesia, the Philippines, and Vietnam (IEEFA 2021). Some believe that coal buyouts are not cost-effective and that countries should use resources to invest in renewable energy instead (Del Bello 2021). Yet the cost of buying coal plants could be partially offset by repurposing plants into solar plus battery systems. A study for India found that such a setup could outweigh the cost of decommissioning fivefold (IEEFA 2020). Buyout plans may also face political-economy constraints, as many power plants are controlled by state-owned enterprises whose operators may be reluctant to give up control. Any such deal would also have to assist in retraining the plants' workforce. For example, nearly half a million people in India currently work in the coal sector, one of the reasons the government is finding it particularly hard to negotiate its exit (Del Bello 2021).

A second type of subsidy aims to spur firms' green innovation by encouraging investments in R&D, skills training, and energy-efficient capital upgrades. Such types of government support may be warranted in the presence of knowledge externalities, which create a gap between the private and social returns of producing knowledge, which typically leads to underinvestment in knowledge-intensive activities (World Bank 2012). Governments could also address coordination failures within and across industries, as the comparative advantage in one sector may depend on another activity in the country (Murphy, Shleifer, and Vishny 1989; Okuno-Fujiwara 1988; Pack and Westphal 1986; Rodenstein-Rodan 1943; Trindade 2005). For example, for Morocco to develop its concentrated solar industry, it also has to create the energy demand, the needed transmission lines, and the domestic supply chains (such as mirrors) to develop and sustain this sector (World Bank 2012). A government's commitments to cofinance some initial activities can act as the precommitment mechanism and solve the prerequisites problem (Rodrik 2004). The same argument often holds for green policies that aim to support new industrial activities by increasing skilled workers, technology adoption, or infrastructure provision (Harrison and Rodríguez-Clare 2009).

Countries should adjust their green innovation policy to be based on their level of capacity. Countries use a variety of programs to develop domestic know-how and support low-carbon innovation. The most technologically advanced countries tend to combine innovation and environmental policies to support frontier innovation. For example, Canada has advanced programs in place to support entrepreneurs in developing breakthrough technologies and solutions to reduce GHG emissions (OECD 2022). Developing countries tend to focus on policies that promote catch-up innovation and the adoption and spread of suitably adapted technologies and policies that improve domestic absorptive capacity, including strengthening local skills (World Bank 2012). Examples of support include technical assistance to improve energy efficiency (Morocco and Uzbekistan), reduce waste (Tunisia), or offer designated training and skills development initiatives tailored to green technologies (Costa Rica and Jordan) (OECD 2022).

Governments also aim to stimulate green technology transfers by subsidizing links with MNEs. As illustrated in chapter 2 of this book, in many sectors the bulk of MNEs' impacts on emissions originates from their supply chains. Encouraging foreign investors to engage with sustainable suppliers and partners, both locally and in their foreign operations, can thus support emissions reduction objectives (OECD 2022). At the same time, greater interaction with multinationals can encourage domestic firms to monitor better, engage in target setting, and take more action to reduce their carbon emissions. These types of spillovers can occur through different types of engagement, including supply links, technology licensing, and joint ventures. In some cases, this would warrant direct types of support (such as tax incentives or subsidies) to encourage both domestic firms and MNEs to take up such links.

To create these links with MNEs, support may also be needed to upgrade the absorptive capacity of local firms. A key requirement for spillovers to materialize is that local businesses have sufficient absorptive capacity to meet the demands of foreign investors. This may require a type of government support to help local firms upgrade their capital equipment and workforce (OECD 2015). An example of such a "supplier development program" to stimulate green technology spillovers comes from Türkiye, where the government invited domestic firms to participate in a 24-month project to help produce parts for electric and hybrid automotive vehicle production of specific MNEs. Such support may thus improve the capacity of local firms, while simultaneously shifting them to a more sustainable automotives industry (Saurav and Viney 2021).

Governments can provide incentives to attract FDI in green sectors. If the local presence of MNEs can result in green technology transfers to domestic firms (see chapter 3), then there could be large social benefits from their relocation to the host country. However, because FDI is more mobile across countries than domestic firms, it may require offering some (temporary) subsidies to attract MNEs to the country. Jointly, this provides a classic case where (tax) incentives could result in net social benefits (Margalioth 2003; Zolt 2013). Such incentives have become more ubiquitous in developing countries in recent years (Andersen, Kett, and Uexkull 2018). However, the impact of incentives on FDI is more mixed, often resulting in little or no new investment (IMF et al. 2015). James (2013) further shows that tax incentives are eight times more effective in attracting FDI for countries with good investment climates. Gondor and Nistor (2012) thus conclude that "a low tax burden cannot compensate for a generally weak or unattractive FDI environment." Yet, incentives can often play a role in the final negotiation stage between investors and governments of shortlisted investment locations (Freund and Moran 2017).

Governments are increasingly adopting support for green investors. Policy makers offer different types of support to attract investors with high green innovation potentials. Examples include incubators and technology parks in Canada (Net Zero Accelerator), Costa Rica (Green Tech Incubator), and Morocco (Green Energy Park). These all serve as ways to attract green FDI and offer platforms for researching, developing, testing, and rolling out low-carbon technologies and processes (OECD 2022). Kronfol, Steenbergen, and Kett (forthcoming) show that green tax incentives are also growing in scale. Governments are increasingly competing to attract the same type of low-carbon industries (such as battery production and electric vehicles). This could risk a race to the bottom, where firms have so many competing offers that their original location decisions are unaffected but the host government now has to offer expensive subsidies.

Many governments also continue to use subsidies to encourage harmful activities. Some countries also have financial incentives in place that subsidize consumption and investment in polluting sectors, such as fossil fuels. Box 5.4 provides an example of this for Ghana, which had both disincentives and incentives for polluting industries, indicating a conflicting policy on its green agenda. More broadly, subsidies for polluting sectors still abound. In 2019, consumer subsidies on fossil fuels amounted to 2 times the spending on development aid, 7 times the combined global carbon prices, and 33 times the pledges made to the Green Climate Fund to assist developing countries in climate change mitigation and adaptation practices (OECD 2022). Phasing out such measures is essential to ensure that the overall system of investment incentives is coherent with green growth goals (OECD 2015).

Persuasion (Corporate Commitments, Information Campaigns)

A final approach to shape the behavior of MNEs is found in the softer approach aimed at encouraging firms to shift their behavior through persuasion and information campaigns. These approaches are often adopted when there is no political support to impose regulatory or price-based instruments or when such instruments are ill suited to the problem. Public disclosure helps reduce the information asymmetry between firms, government, and consumers. In doing so, it can improve environmental performance through various channels (Blackman, Afsah, and Ratunanda 2004; Powers et al. 2011; Tietenberg 1998; World Bank 2012):

- **Output market pressure:** Affect demand for firms' products
- **Input market pressure:** Affect demand for publicly traded companies' shares and the ability of such companies to hire and retain employees
- **Judicial pressure:** Encourage private citizens to sue polluters
- **Regulatory pressure:** Build support for new pollution control legislation or more stringent enforcement of existing legislation
- **Community pressure:** Enhance pressure from community groups and nongovernmental organizations

BOX 5.4 How Green Are Tax Incentives in Ghana?

In 2022, the World Bank reviewed Ghana's tax incentives regime for its Climate Change and Development Report. This analysis is based on the World Bank Global Corporate Tax Incentives Database (under development, unpublished), which systematically captures information on tax parameter and corporate income tax incentives.[a]

The analysis finds that Ghana has not offered any corporate income tax incentive with an explicit environmental objective since 2009, but the government has more broadly been offering some tax incentives that support green sectors.

- Between 2009 and 2015, the government offered a seven-year tax holiday for firms in the waste processing sector, which subsequently evolved to a reduced corporate tax rate of 1 percent.
- Since 2017, young entrepreneurs operating in the energy production and waste processing sectors can qualify for a five-year tax holiday followed by a five-year reduced tax rate of 5 to 15 percent.
- Other countries in the region also offer tax incentives for green sectors. For example, Zimbabwe offers immediate depreciation for expenditures on water conservation works and prevention of soil erosion, and Angola offers a reduced tax rate and accelerated depreciation in waste processing and reforestation.

For polluting industries, Ghana has disincentives and incentives, indicating a conflicting policy on the green agenda. These contradictory tax measures to the same sectors likely offset most potential environmental gains.

- As disincentives, the extractives sector faces a higher statutory corporate income tax rate of 35 percent compared to the 25 percent standard corporate income tax rate. Mining support services also pay an additional tax of 5 percent (National Fiscal Stabilization levy), while assets in extractives sectors also have slower depreciation rates.
- As incentives, however, mineral companies with a government investment agreement are not bound by the higher corporate income tax rate. Instead, they pay a reduced rate (as per the agreement terms) and can carry losses forward as per the agreement terms.
- This inconsistent combination of disincentives and incentives for polluting sectors is also found in some other African countries. For example, in 2019/2020, Ethiopia, Nigeria, and South Africa were imposing higher statutory corporate income tax rates on at least parts of the extractives sector, while simultaneously offering incentives to extractive subsectors through tax holidays and reduced rates.

Source: World Bank 2022.

a. As of January 2022, the database covers 40 countries over the years 2009 to 2019/2020. Seven countries, which constitute the regional comparators referenced in this analysis, are in Sub-Saharan Africa—namely, Angola, Democratic Republic of Congo, Côte d'Ivoire, Ethiopia, Ghana, Mauritius, South Africa, and Zimbabwe.

- **Managerial information:** Provide data to managers about their pollution and options to reduce it

Persuasion and information campaigns have proven successful in limiting environmental pollution. Regulations requiring US electric utilities to mail bill inserts to consumers reporting the extent of their reliance on fossil fuels led to a significant decrease in companies' fossil fuel use (Delmas, Montes-Sancho, and Shimshack 2007). A policy of publicly disclosing the identity of noncompliant plants ("naming-and-shaming") spurred emissions reductions in a sample of pulp and paper plants in British Columbia, Canada (Foulon, Lanoie, and Laplante 2002). Similarly, some programs run by civil society organizations encourage enforcement of environmental regulations where formal institutions are weak by evaluating and rating plants' environmental performance. Examples include China's GreenWatch program; India's Green Rating Project; Indonesia's Program for Pollution Control, Evaluation, and Rating (PROPER); the Philippines' EcoWatch program; and Vietnam's Black and Green Books initiative (World Bank 2012). Examples of different approaches for persuasion include the following:

- Corporate commitment campaigns to reduce carbon-intensive activities (scale)
- Eco-certification to encourage firms to adopt low-carbon approaches (technology)
- ESG standards and impact investing to reduce borrowing costs of green projects (technology)
- Green investment promotion and facilitation (composition)

Corporate commitment campaigns can be a powerful way to target a small number of firms to rapidly encourage sustainability standards that affect very large numbers of producers in their value chain. To attain scale in the climate change transition, targeting large MNEs can be extremely effective. Such companies are particularly attuned to public concerns and exquisitely sensitive to risks to their valuable brands, and can stimulate a "race to the top." For example, two large supermarkets—Whole Foods and Sainsbury's—became early adopters of only sourcing sustainable seafood certified by the Marine Stewardship Council. Next, Walmart announced that it would also shift its purchasing and sparked a surge in fisheries seeking certification, creating a clear inflection point in growth in the Marine Stewardship Council's market share. Similarly, when an international campaign pushed several smaller companies to only source sustainable forestry in their supply chains, this inspired the two largest players—Cargill and Wilmar—to make similar commitments to protect their brands (Mandle et al. 2019). Due to their economically dominant role within supply chains, the actions of these MNEs can thus impose sustainability standards that affect millions of producers in some cases (Thorlakson, Zegher, and Lambin 2018). Governments can encourage such behavior by monitoring MNEs climate commitments or even actively persuading MNEs to adopt more ambitious climate commitments.

Another opportunity for encouraging firms to adopt more green practices comes through encouraging eco-certification. Some consumers choose to pay extra to purchase products of superior environmental quality. Companies—motivated by a price premium, consumer loyalty, or brand differentiation—choose to supply such products and contribute to maintaining or enhancing ecosystem services (often certified by third parties). This creates demand for firms to shift to less polluting technologies. For example, Costa Rica's Certification for Sustainable Tourism program was one of the first performance-based voluntary environmental programs created and allowed hotels with higher environmental performance to establish price premiums (Rivera 2002). Similarly, the Rainforest Alliance certification led to enhanced tree cover and greater landscape connectivity in Colombia (Rueda, Thomas, and Lambin 2015) and in Ethiopia increased the probability of forest conservation by 20 percent relative to areas lacking certification (Takahashi and Todo 2013). Governments who encourage eco-certification can thus stimulate firms' environmental outcomes.

Impact investing is another market-oriented mechanism to encourage green investment. Forms of sustainable finance have grown rapidly in recent years, as a growing number of institutional investors now pursue ESG investing approaches. This growth has been spurred by shifts in demand from across the finance ecosystem, driven by both the search for better long-term financial value and a pursuit of better alignment with values. For impact investing, consumers of a financial product pay into an investment vehicle that is designed to generate both financial returns and ecosystem service benefits. Consumers of a financial product pay into an investment vehicle in anticipation of both financial and environmental returns. Firms often benefit by receiving a concessionary rate of borrowing in exchange for the environmental and social co-benefits (Mandle et al. 2019). The ESG system still faces problems with monitoring firms' actual climate impact (see chapter 2 and "MNEs' Commitments to Net-Zero Emissions by 2050" in chapter 4). Yet, in its basis it has potential to correct market failures: where the traditional markets are not adequately capturing the value provided by ecosystems, new markets are set up to allow consumers to bear some of the costs or risks of securing or enhancing ecosystem services (Mandle et al. 2019).

Finally, governments can also promote and attract low-carbon FDI through their investment promotion agencies (IPAs). These IPAs are key players in bridging information gaps that otherwise hinder the attraction of FDI and their potential sustainable development impacts. IPAs' primary role is to create awareness of existing investment opportunities, attract investors, and facilitate their establishment and expansion in the economy, including by linking them to potential local partners (OECD 2022). A significant body of literature confirms that the activities of IPAs attract FDI in their targeted sectors (Harding and Javorcik 2011; Steenbergen, forthcoming). Since few economies can offer an attractive environment for all low-carbon technologies, IPAs should review and identify specific economic activities where they see a potential to develop low-carbon activities or growth poles. On this basis they can design investment promotion packages combining a variety of tools that range from intelligence gathering (for example, market studies) and sector-specific events (inward and outward missions) to proactive investor engagement (one-to-one meetings, email and phone campaigns, inquiry handling) (OECD 2022).

IPAs can also support the carbon transition through investment facilitation and aftercare services. Facilitation services help reduce administrative barriers to low-carbon investment. IPAs are often the first point of contact for foreign investors and can thereby support them in acquiring the necessary permits and clearances to enter and operate in the country by guiding them through the required procedures and facilitating access to relevant government bodies. Aftercare services, in turn, help firms that are already established in the country overcome any information barriers or regulatory constraints related to reinvestment or to establish supplier links. IPAs could therefore help MNEs identify low-carbon business partners, suppliers, and distributors, and help them reduce emissions along their supply chains. This could also encourage green technology spillovers (OECD 2022).

How to Prioritize and Sequence the 5Ps within a Climate Change Mitigation Strategy

In shaping their climate change mitigation strategies, governments should seek to prioritize those activities that shape MNE behaviors to maximize local and immediate benefits and avoid lock-in. As mentioned throughout this report, the actions of MNEs should play a central role in many countries' climate change mitigation strategies due to (a) MNEs' ability to impose sustainability standards on their supply chains that affect millions of producers and (b) their potential to provide green technology spillovers for local firms. The 5Ps framework provides a helpful way to identify the various types of instruments available to governments to affect the impact of MNEs on climate change. However, this does not provide any guidance on prioritization or sequencing. To guide policy makers on operationalizing this framework, it is helpful to consider the principles that define good climate change policy more broadly, as defined by World Bank (2012): maximizing local benefits and avoiding lock-ins.

Maximize local and immediate benefits and synergies with other development objectives. Climate change mitigation strategy should aim to minimize transition costs for private sector stakeholders by offsetting them (to the extent possible) with visible and immediate benefits. World Bank (2012) calls on developing countries (especially low-income countries) to prioritize one of three policies: (a) policies that have a negative or zero economic cost thanks to synergies with development (for example, hydropower), (b) policies that have a positive economic cost but large direct welfare impacts (for example, reducing local air pollution or climate risks), or (c) policies that are financed from external sources (for example, through carbon trading). In the case of MNEs, this means taking extra care to attract green FDI that could facilitate the energy transition while also generate additional jobs. It also means encouraging green technology transfers that would help local firms use more energy-efficient production methods and safeguarding the economy's long-term green competitiveness. This further creates momentum for climate change reform and builds the necessary political space for more difficult, costly transitions down the road (for example, related to more ambitious climate change policies such as binding emissions standards and energy taxes).

Avoid lock-ins, where a delay in action increases the cost of achieving the same end point. Governments cannot adopt all reforms simultaneously; they have limited resources, institutional capacity, and political capital to devote to complex problems. Policy makers should thus prioritize those activities that would increase the cost of achieving the same point. This calls for a focus on the sectors and interventions that are most urgent. An obvious example could be avoiding foreign investment in new coal power plants, which would directly increase emissions but may also attract other energy-intensive polluting industries, thus further raising the cost for the country to shift toward a net-zero emissions economy by 2050.

Jointly these two principles provide guidance on how to prioritize and sequence activities (table 5.2). First, activities that have clear development synergies and are urgent should be prioritized. Examples of this could include environmental disclosure laws to monitor emissions of MNEs and their supply chains (that guide other policies and avoid lock-ins to more carbon intensive activities). Second, activities that have

TABLE 5.2 Synergy versus Urgency in Using the 5Ps Framework

Potential for synergies or trade-offs	Urgency of the initiative	
	Urgent (A delay in action increases the cost of achieving the same end point.)	**Less urgent (A delay in action does not increase in cost of achieving the same end point.)**
Synergies (Action facilitates the achievement of other development objectives.)	Prioritize. Synergetic and urgent actions should be part of the recommendations. *Example: environmental disclosure laws to monitor emissions of MNEs and their supply chain*	Implement if capacity allows. Delay action if too complex, or benefits uncertain. *Example: incentives to stimulate green technology transfers from MNEs to domestic firms*
Trade-offs (The cost of action makes the achievement of other development objectives more difficult.)	Adopt with care. Options to explore include (a) specific designs to minimize trade-offs and (b) adopting a complementary agenda. *Example: global environmental standards enforcement that encourages changes in production methods for MNEs and their supply chains*	Delay. Actions with major economic trade-offs that can be delayed, should be delayed. *Example: environmental taxes that may raise energy prices in short-run and scare off foreign direct investment.*

Source: World Bank based on World Bank 2012.
Note: MNEs = multinational enterprises.

development synergies but are less urgent should be implemented if capacity allows. Examples here include any policies to stimulate green technology transfers from MNEs to domestic firms. Third, activities with significant trade-offs but that are urgent should be adopted with care. Examples include the local adoption of global environmental standards to encourage changes in production methods for MNEs and their supply chains. While important, this runs the risk of undermining a large share of less-productive domestic firms and so may need to be adopted with a complementary agenda. Finally, actions with major economic trade-offs that can be delayed, should be delayed. An example would be overly ambitious environmental taxes that may raise energy prices in the short-run and scare off FDI.

Finally, there is need for an active research agenda that further defines how to prioritize, sequence, and implement economic policy to shape the climate change activities of MNEs. This report has provided an overview of some of the latest literature, data, and economic analysis on the various challenges and opportunities that MNEs bring to climate change mitigation. It has also touched on the various policy instruments available to policy makers in shaping this dynamic, via the 5Ps framework and their relationship to the scope, technology, and composition effects of MNEs. However, there is still much that is unclear, most notably on how many of these instruments complement each other (for example, patrolling is likely a critical foundation for much of the other 5Ps), or how instruments are substitutes (as regulations, taxes, and

BOX 5.5 Future Research Agenda—The Specific Use and Complementarities of Policies to Shape the Impacts of MNEs on Climate Change

This chapter touched on a range of policy instruments available to policy makers in shaping the impacts of multinational enterprises (MNEs) on climate change via the 5Ps framework and the instruments' relationship to the scope, technology, and composition effects of MNEs. However, climate action and achieving impact through government programs require a more nuanced understanding of the mechanisms of effect and the contextual suitability of the 5Ps. Various knowledge deficiencies prevent such advancements, including the following:

- What insights can be gleaned from the policy responses being adopted by developed and developing countries for climate change mitigation and adaptation?
- To what extent do these policy instruments complement each other (for example, patrolling is likely an important foundation for much for much of the other 5Ps)?
- To what extent can instruments be substitutes in realizing similar objectives by affecting levers for behavior change? That is, do regulations, taxes and subsidies offer different ways to reach the same goal, which is typically a change in agent behavior?

Toward this end, a database that sources global information and is organized per the 5Ps framework could be value adding for policy researchers as well as policy makers.

Source: World Bank.

subsidies offer different ways to reach the same goal). This is an active research agenda that will be critical going forward (see box 5.5) to best guide policy makers on realizing the climate change transition by shaping the activities of MNEs.

Notes

1. In 2013, an eight-story commercial building called Rana Plaza collapsed in Bangladesh, resulting in over 1,100 deaths and approximately 2,500 injuries. It is considered the deadliest garment-factory disaster in history and the deadliest industrial accident in the history of Bangladesh. This resulted in a large backlash against global garment brands, many of whom had subcontracted production of their clothes to the Rana Plaza factories.
2. ESG criteria are a set of standards for a company's behavior used by socially conscious investors to screen potential investments.
3. OECD (Organisation for Economic Co-operation and Development), OECD Glossary of Statistical Terms, "environmental taxes," https://stats.oecd.org/glossary/.
4. Appropriate compensation policies will vary with circumstances of lower-income households in each country. Mechanisms can include targeted transfers to poorer households (for example, cash-transfer systems). Alternatively, public spending could be increased on policies disproportionately benefiting the poor, such as housing support or public health care (Pigato 2019).

References

Ambec, S., M. A. Cohen, S. Elgie, and P. Lanoie. 2011. "The Porter Hypothesis at 20: Can Environmental Regulation Enhance Innovation and Competitiveness?" Discussion Paper 11-01, Resources for the Future, Washington, DC.

Andersen, Maria R., Benjamin R. Kett, and Erik von Uexkull. 2018. "Corporate Tax Incentives and FDI in Developing Countries." In *Global Investment Competitiveness Report 2017/2018: Foreign Investor Perspectives and Policy Implications*, World Bank Group, 73–99. Washington, DC: World Bank.

Baumol, W., and W. Oates. 1988. *The Theory of Environmental Policy*. 2nd ed. Cambridge: Cambridge University Press.

Berestycki, Clara, and Antoine Dechezleprêtre. 2020. "Assessing the Efficiency of Environmental Policy Design and Evaluation: Results from a 2018 Cross-Country Survey." Organisation for Economic Co-operation and Development (OECD) Economics Department Working Paper 1611, OECD, Paris. https://www.oecd-ilibrary.org/economics/assessing-the-efficiency-of-environmental-policy-design-and-evaluation-results-from-a-2018-cross-country-survey_482f8fbe-en.

Bingler, J. A., M. Kraus, M. Leippold, and N. Webersinke. 2022. "Cheap Talk and Cherry-Picking: What ClimateBert Has to Say on Corporate Climate Risk Disclosures." *Finance Research Letters* 47 (B). https://doi.org/10.1016/j.frl.2022.102776.

Blackman, A., S. Afsah, and D. Ratunanda. 2004."How Does Public Disclosure Work? Evidence from Indonesia's PROPER Program." *Human Ecology Review* 11 (3): 235–46.

Bolton, Patrick, and Marcin T. Kacperczyk. 2022. "Firm Commitments." Columbia Business School Research Paper, New York.

Borghesi, S., C. Franco, and G. Marin. 2020. "Outward Foreign Direct Investment Patterns of Italian Firms in the European Union's Emissions Trading Scheme." *Scandinavian Journal of Economics* 122 (1): 219–56. https://doi.org/10.1111/sjoe.12323.

Brenton, Paul, and Vicky Chemutai. 2021. *The Trade and Climate Change Nexus: The Urgency and Opportunities for Developing Countries*. Washington, DC: World Bank. https://openknowledge.worldbank.org/handle/10986/36294.

Cohen, Mark, and Adeline Tubb. 2018. "The Impact of Environmental Regulation on Firm and Country Competitiveness: A Meta-Analysis of the Porter Hypothesis." *Journal of the Association of Environmental and Resource Economists* 5 (2): 371–99. https://www.journals.uchicago.edu/doi/abs/10.1086/695613.

Cole, Matthew A. 2004. "Trade, the Pollution Haven Hypothesis, and the Environmental Kuznets Curve: Examining the Linkages." *Ecological Economics* 48 (1): 71–81. https://www.sciencedirect.com/science/article/abs/pii/S0921800903002556.

Copeland, B. R. 2012. "International Trade and Green Growth." Paper presented at the Green Growth Knowledge Platform inaugural conference, Mexico City, January 12–13.

Copeland, Brian, and M. Scott Taylor. 1994. "North-South Trade and the Environment." *Quarterly Journal of Economics* 109 (3): 755–87. https://www.jstor.org/stable/2118421?seq=1#metadata_info_tab_contents.

Dam, Lammertjan, and Bert Scholtens. 2008. "Environmental Regulation and MNEs Location: Does CSR Matter?" *Ecological Economics* 67 (1): 55–65. https://www.sciencedirect.com/science/article/abs/pii/S0921800907005356.

Del Bello, Lou. 2021. "Asian Development Bank Plans to Buy Out and Retire Coal Plants." *The Third Pole*, October 11, 2021. https://www.thethirdpole.net/en/climate/asian-development-bank-plans-buy-out-retire-coal-plants/.

Delmas, M., M. Montes-Sancho, and J. Shimshack. 2007. "Information Disclosure Policies: Evidence from the Electricity Industry." Working paper, Department of Economics, Tufts University, Medford and Somerville, MA.

Dinan, Terry. 2015. "Offsetting a Carbon Tax's Burden on Low-Income Households." In *Implementing a US Carbon Tax*, edited by Ian Parry, Adele Morris, and Roberton Williams III. Abingdon, UK: Routledge.

Foulon J., P. Lanoie, and B. Laplante. 2002."Incentives for Pollution Control: Regulation or Information?" *Journal of Environmental Economics and Management* 44 (1): 169–87.

Franke, Andreas. 2021. "Dutch Government Agrees on Closure Compensation for 731-MW Rotterdam Coal Plant." SP Global, December 1, 2021. https://www.spglobal.com/commodityinsights/en/market-insights/latest-news/electric-power/120121-dutch-government-agrees-on-closure-compensation-for-731-mw-rotterdam-coal-plant.

Freund, C., and T. H. Moran. 2017. "Multinational Investors as Export Superstars: How Emerging-Market Governments Can Reshape Comparative Advantage." Working Paper 17-1, Peterson Institute for International Economics, Washington, DC.

Gardner, T. A., M. Benzie, J. Börner, E. Dawkins, S. Fick, R. Garrett, J. Godar, A. Grimard, S. Lake, R. K. Larsen, N. Mardas, C. L. McDermott, P. Meyfroidt, M. Osbeck, M. Persson, T. Sembres, C. Suavet, B. Strassburg, A. Trevisan, C. West, and P. Wolvekamp. 2018. "Transparency and Sustainability in Global Commodity Supply Chains." *World Development* 121: 163–77. https://doi.org/10.1016/j.worlddev.2018.05.025.

Gast, Johanna, Katherine Gundolf, and Beate Cesinger. 2017. "Doing Business in a Green Way: A Systematic Review of the Ecological Sustainability Entrepreneurship Literature and Future Research Directions." *Journal of Cleaner Production* 147 (March): 44–56. https://www.sciencedirect.com/science/article/abs/pii/S0959652617300720.

Gondor, M. and P. Nistor. 2012. "Does High Corporate Tax Rates Attract Foreign Direct Investment?" Ovidius University Annals, Economic Sciences Series, Ovidius University of Constantza, Faculty of Economic Sciences, vol. 0(1), pages 1433-1438, May.

Grossman, G. M., and A. G. Kruger. 1991. "Environmental Influences of a North American Free Trade Agreement." NBER Working paper 3914, National Bureau of Economic Research, Cambridge, MA.

Haldar, Stuti. 2019. "Towards a Conceptual Understanding of Sustainability-Driven Entrepreneurship." *Corporate Social Responsibility and Environmental Management* 26 (6): 1157–70. https://onlinelibrary.wiley.com/doi/abs/10.1002/csr.1763.

Harding, Torfinn, and Beata S. Javorcik. 2011. "Roll Out the Red Carpet and They Will Come: Investment Promotion and FDI Inflows." *Economic Journal* 121 (557): 1445–76.

Harrington, Winston, Richard D. Morgenstern, and Peter Nelson. 1999. "On the Accuracy of Regulatory Cost Estimates," Discussion Paper 99-18, Resources for the Future, Washington, DC.

Harrison, A., and A. Rodríguez-Clare. 2009."Trade, Foreign Investment, and Industrial Policy for Developing Countries." In *Handbook for Development Economics*, edited by D. Rodrik and M. Rosenzweig, vol. 5, 4039–214. Amsterdam: North-Holland.

Holland, S. P. 2009. "Taxes and Trading versus Intensity Standards: Second-Best Environmental Policies with Incomplete Regulation. Leakage or Market Power?" NBER Working Paper 15262, National Bureau of Economic Research, Cambridge, MA.

IEEFA (Institute for Energy Economics and Financial Analysis). 2020. "IEEFA: Repurposing Coal Plants into Solar and Battery Can Pay Up to 5 Times More Than Decommissioning." IEEFA, Lakewood, OH. https://ieefa.org/articles/ieefa-repurposing-coal-plants-solar-and-battery-can-pay-5-times-more-decommissioning.

IEEFA (Institute for Energy Economics and Financial Analysis). 2021. "ADB Backs Coal Power Retirement In Southeast Asia—New Program Targets the Right Issues, but More Solutions May Be Needed." IEEFA, Lakewood, OH.

IMF (International Monetary Fund), OECD (Organisation for Economic Co-operation and Development), UN (United Nations), and World Bank. 2015. "Options for Low Income Countries' Effective and Efficient Use of Tax Incentives for Investment: A Report to the G-20 Development Working Group by the IMF, OECD, UN and World Bank." World Bank, Washington, DC.

James, S. 2013. "Tax and Non-Tax Incentives and Investments: Evidence and Policy Implications." Investment Climate Advisory Services, World Bank, Washington, DC.

Johnson, Matthew P., and Stefan Schaltegger. 2019. "Entrepreneurship for Sustainable Development: A Review and Multilevel Causal Mechanism Framework." *Entrepreneurship Theory and Practice* 44 (6): 1141–73. https://journals.sagepub.com/doi/10.1177/1042258719885368.

Kalkuhl, M., O. Edenhofer, and K. Lessmann. 2011. "Learning or Lock-In: Optimal Technology Policies to Support Mitigation." CESufi Working Paper Series No. 3422. Munich: CESifo Group.

Kim, Eun-Hee, and Thomas Lyon. 2011. "Strategic Environmental Disclosure: Evidence from the DOE's Voluntary Greenhouse Gas Registry." *Journal of Environmental Economics and Management* 61 (3): 311–26. https://www.sciencedirect.com/science/article/pii/S0095069610001075.

Kim, Yeseul, and Dong-Eun Rhee. 2019. "Do Stringent Environmental Regulations Attract Foreign Direct Investment in Developing Countries? Evidence on the 'Race to the Top' from Cross-Country Panel Data." *Emerging Markets Finance and Trade* 55 (12): 2796–808. https://www.tandfonline.com/doi/full/10.1080/1540496X.2018.1531240?scroll=top&need-Access=true.

Koźluk, Tomasz, and Christina Timiliotis. 2016. "Do Environmental Policies Affect Global Value Chains? A New Perspective on the Pollution Haven Hypothesis." Organisation for Economic Co-operation and Development (OECD) Economics Department Working Paper 1282, OECD, Paris. https://www.oecd-ilibrary.org/content/paper/5jm2hh7nf3wd-en?crawler=true.

Koźluk, Tomasz. 2014. "The Indicators of the Economic Burdens of Environmental Policy Design: Results from the OECD Questionnaire." Organisation for Economic Co-operation and

Development (OECD) Economics Department Working Paper 1178, OECD, Paris. https://www.oecd-ilibrary.org/content/paper/5jxrjnbnbm8v-en.

Kronfol, Hania, Victor Steenbergen, and Ben Kett. Forthcoming. "Green Corporate Tax Incentives." World Bank, Washington, DC.

Kusek, Peter, Abhishek Saurav, and Ryan Kuo. 2020. "Outlook and Priorities for Foreign Investors in Developing Countries: Findings from the 2019 Global Investment Competitiveness Survey in 10 Middle-Income Countries." In *Global Investment Competitiveness Report 2019/2020: Rebuilding Investor Confidence in Times of Uncertainty,* edited by World Bank Group, 24–54. Washington, DC: World Bank. http://pubdocs.worldbank.org/en/314571591134463825/211536-Chapter-1.pdf.

Mandle, L., Z. Ouyang, J. Salzman, and G. C. Daily. 2019. *Green Growth That Works: Natural Capital Policy and Finance Mechanisms around the World.* Washington, DC: Island Press.

Margalioth, Y. 2003. "Tax Competition, Foreign Direct Investments and Growth: Using the Tax System to Promote Developing Countries." *Virginia Tax Review* 23: 161.

Murphy, K. M., A. Shleifer, and R. W. Vishny. 1989. "Industrialization and the Big Push." *Journal of Political Economy* 97 (5): 1003–26.

OECD (Organisation for Economic Co-operation and Development). 2015. *Aligning Policies for a Low-Carbon Economy.* Paris: OECD Publishing. https://doi.org/10.1787/9789264233294-en.

OECD (Organisation for Economic Co-operation and Development). 2022. *FDI Qualities Policy Toolkit.* Paris: OECD Publishing. https://doi.org/10.1787/7ba74100-en.

Okuno-Fujiwara, M. 1988. "Interdependence of Industries, Coordination Failure, and Strategic Promotion of an Industry." *Journal of International Economics* 25 (1/2): 25–43.

Omri, Anis, Duc Khuong Nguyen, and Christopher Rault. 2014. "Causal Interactions between CO_2 Emissions, FDI, and Economic Growth: Evidence from Dynamic Simultaneous-Equation Models." *Economic Modelling* 42: 382–89. https://www.sciencedirect.com/science/article/abs/pii/S0264999314002818.

Pack, H., and L. E. Westphal. 1986. "Industrial Strategy and Technological Change" *Journal of Development Economics* 22 (1): 87–128.

Parry, Ian, Victor Mylonas, and Nate Vernon. 2017. "Reforming Energy Policy in India: Assessing the Options." Working Paper 2017/103, International Monetary Fund, Washington, DC. https://doi.org/10.5089/9781475595734.001.

Pigato, Miria A., ed. 2019. *Fiscal Policies for Development and Climate Action.* International Development in Focus. Washington, DC: World Bank. https://doi.org/10.1596/978-1-4648-1358-0.

Ploeg, Matthias, Carlos Hinojosa, and Michal Miedzinski. 2017. *The Search for Synergy: Business Environment Reform and Green Growth. Green Growth Working Group.* https://www.greengrowth-knowledge.org/resource/search-synergy-business-environment-reform-and-green-growth.

Poelhekke, Steven, and Rick van der Ploeg. 2015. "Green Havens and Pollution Havens." *World Economy* 38 (7): 1159–78.

Powers, N., A. Blackman, T. Lyon, and U. Narain. 2011. "Does Disclosure Reduce Pollution? Evidence from India's Green Rating Project." *Environmental & Resource Economics* 50 (1): 131–55.

Richter, W. F., and K. Schneider. 2003. "Energy Taxation: Reasons for Discriminating in Favor of the Production Sector." *European Economic Review* 47 (3): 461–76.

Rivera, J. 2002. "Assessing a Voluntary Environmental Initiative in the Developing World: The Costa Rican Certification for Sustainable Tourism." *Policy Sciences* 35: 333–60.

Rivera, Jorge, and Chang Hoon Oh. 2013. "Environmental Regulations and Multinational Enterprises' Foreign Market Entry Investments." *Policy Studies Journal* 41 (2): 243–72. https://onlinelibrary.wiley.com/doi/abs/10.1111/psj.12016.

Rodenstein-Rodan, P. N. 1943. "Problems of Industrialization of Eastern and Southeastern Europe." *Economic Journal* 53: 202–11.

Rodrik, D. 2004. "Industrial Policy for the Twenty-First Century." Available at SSRN 666808.

Rueda, X., N. E. Thomas, and E. F. Lambin. 2015. "Eco-Certification and Coffee Cultivation Enhance Tree Cover and Forest Connectivity in the Colombian Coffee Landscapes." *Regional Environmental Change* 15 (1): 25–33.

Saurav, Abhishek, and Brody Viney. 2021. "Catalyzing Investment for Green Growth." Equitable Growth, Finance and Institutions Insight. World Bank, Washington, DC.

Shahbaz, Muhammad, Samia Nasreen, Faisal Abbas, and Omri Anis. 2015. "Does Foreign Direct Investment Impede Environmental Quality in High-, Middle-, and Low-Income Countries?" *Energy Economics* 51 (September): 275–87. https://www.sciencedirect.com/science/article/pii/S0140988315001905.

Steenbergen, Victor. Forthcoming. "What Makes an Investment Promotion Agency Effective: Findings from a Structural Gravity Model." World Bank, Washington DC.

Takahashi, R., and Y. Todo. 2013. "The Impact of a Shade Coffee Certification Program on Forest Conservation: A Case Study from a Wild Coffee Forest in Ethiopia." *Journal of Environmental Management* 130 (C): 48–54.

TCFD (Task Force on Climate-related Financial Disclosures). 2021. "Task Force on Climate-Related Financial Disclosures: Overview." https://assets.bbhub.io/company/sites/60/2020/10/TCFD_Booklet_FNL_Digital_March-2020.pdf.

Thaler, R. H., and C. R. Sunstein. 2008. *Nudge: Improving Decisions about Health, Wealth, and Happiness.* New Haven, CT: Yale University Press.

Thorlakson, T., J. F. de Zegher, and E. F. Lambin. 2018. "Companies' Contribution to Sustainability through Global Supply Chains." *Proceedings of the National Academy of Sciences* 115 (9): 2072–77. https://doi.org/10.1073/pnas.1716695115

Tietenberg, T. H. 1998. *Environmental Economics and Policy.* Boston: Addison-Wesley.

Trindade, V. 2005. "The Big Push, Industrialization, and International Trade: The Role of Exports." *Journal of Development Economics* 78 (October): 22–48.

UL Solutions. 2020. "Mandatory Emissions Reporting around the Globe." UL Solutions, August 25, 2020. https://www.ul.com/news/mandatory-emissions-reporting-around-globe.

Vogt-Schilb, A., and S. Hallegatte. 2011. "When Starting with the Most Expensive Option Makes Sense: Use and Misuse of Marginal Abatement Cost Curves." Policy Research Working Paper 5803, World Bank, Washington, DC.

Wade, Robert. 1990. *Governing the Market: Economic Theory and the Role of Government in East Asian Industrialization.* Princeton, NJ: Princeton University Press.

Wilde-Ramsing, Joseph, David Ollivier de Leth, and Manon Wolfkamp. 2021. "The Shell Climate Verdict: A Major Win for Mandatory Due Diligence and Corporate Accountability." Business and Human Rights Resource Centre, June 1, 2021. https://www.business-humanrights.org/en/blog/the-shell-climate-verdict-a-major-win-for-mandatory-due-diligence-and-corporate-accountability/.

World Bank. 2012. *Inclusive Green Growth: The Pathway to Sustainable Development.* Washington, DC: World Bank.

World Bank Group. 2022. "Ghana Country Climate and Development Report." CCDR Series. World Bank, Washington, DC. https://openknowledge.worldbank.org/handle/10986/38209.

Zolt, E. M. 2013. "Tax Incentives and Tax Base Protection Issues." Papers on Selected Topics in Protecting the Tax Base of Developing Countries Draft Paper 3, United Nations, New York.

www.ingramcontent.com/pod-product-compliance
Lightning Source LLC
Chambersburg PA
CBHW041445210326
41599CB00004B/139